THE W... FAITH

Thriving in Your Walk with God

JIM STIER

YWAM PUBLISHING
Seattle, Washington

YWAM Publishing is the publishing ministry of Youth With A Mission (YWAM), an international missionary organization of Christians from many denominations dedicated to presenting Jesus Christ to this generation. To this end, YWAM has focused its efforts in three main areas: (1) training and equipping believers for their part in fulfilling the Great Commission (Matthew 28:19), (2) personal evangelism, and (3) mercy ministry (medical and relief work). For a free catalog of books and materials, call (425) 771-1153 or (800) 922-2143. Visit us online at www.ywampublishing.com.

The Way of Faith: Thriving in Your Walk With God
Copyright © 2019 by Jim Stier

Published by YWAM Publishing
a ministry of Youth With A Mission
P.O. Box 55787, Seattle, WA 98155-0787

Library of Congress Cataloging-in-Publication Data is on file.

ISBN: 978-1-57658-913-7 (paperback)
ISBN: 978-1-57658-671-6 (e-book)

Cover photo: Tiffany Lambert

First printing 2019

Printed in the United States of America

To Pam, my wife and life companion, who was willing to make the journey with me by faith and against all odds, suffering hardship and helping sustain my faith by the strength of hers. Without her I can't imagine how the events spoken of in this book could ever have happened, nor how I would have learned the truths written here.

These are a shadow of the things to come,
but the substance belongs to Christ.
Colossians 2:17 ESV

Contents

Preface 9

Francisco, Part 1 11

   1. Identity 19

   2. Power 31

   3. Obedience 39

Francisco, Part 2 51

   4. Reality 57

   5. Transformation 69

   6. Faith 79

   7. Authenticity 93

Francisco, Part 3 101

   8. Unity 105

   9. Submission and Patience 113

Francisco, Part 4 121

   10. Strategy 125

   11. The Word 133

Francisco, Part 5 139

   12. Miracles 147

   13. Provision 157

   14. Love 169

   Acknowledgments 175

Preface

When Pam and I had just gotten married, God called us to Brazil. We left for that country before we had been married a year and became the founders of Youth With A Mission there. The first years were a constant moving into the impossible. It seemed that God was continually asking us to do something that could not be done without divine intervention. The only way I found to cope with the constantly looming disaster was to seek God and let Him strengthen me. He did that and we survived and progressed. Thousands of Brazilians were mobilized and trained for missions, both long- and short-term.

The understanding for this book came out of those decades of experiencing His provision, both inner and financial. He taught us or we would have failed. He strengthened us or we would have collapsed. He inspired us or we would have lost hope.

Our hearts were enlightened so that we could see and experience the hope of His calling, the riches of His inheritance in the saints, and the exceeding greatness of His power toward us (Eph. 1:18–19).

All of our victories came out of this power and light that He has released in our lives. This is what I've come to understand as living by faith, and it's by living through these things with God that these pages came to be written.

This book is for all who desire to deepen their faith in God, to live out of the power and light God provides. You will encounter parts of my story as well as the story of Francisco, someone who models the power of faith for the twenty-first century.

Francisco, Part 1

In June 1991 a team of six Brazilian missionaries serving with Youth With A Mission went to Angola to live, work, pray, and learn in that proud, war-torn country. Decades of civil war had left a terrible legacy of suffering for the peoples of Angola, and our team determined to help as they could. A cease-fire had gone into effect near the eve of their departure, and there suddenly existed the possibility of helping the starving people of Ganda, a beautiful highlands city situated 250 kilometers inland in the south of the country.

Ganda had been overrun by both armies in thirty years of civil war. The city's infrastructure had been devastated, and eight thousand people had died in the months before our team arrived on the scene. Our little group had worked out a partnership with a German mission. The mission would supply the food and equipment, and the YWAM team would do the work.

This was a work of faith. The leaders, Marcia and Marcos Azolim, were college graduates and full of love, integrity, courage, and faith. The rest of the team didn't have advanced education. Their qualifications were missionary training, a love of Jesus, and a desire to help the people of Angola. The country had been Marxist since independence and was very hesitant about religion. The government extended an invitation to us, though, and the team went.

They were well received by the commissar of Ganda. He laid out a banquet of lobster and invited the most important people

of the region. The Brazilian missionaries weren't used to being
treated like that but soon settled down to enjoy the delicacies.
Most of them had never tasted lobster before. Then the commissar got up to give a welcoming speech. He began, "We're so glad to
have six new doctors here to help our people!"

Our team was stunned. None of them was a doctor. Would
they get kicked out of the country? They hadn't meant to come
on false pretenses. How had the commissar gotten the impression
that they were a medical team?

We never did find out, but the team wasn't asked to leave,
so they settled in to try to save people from dying of starvation.
During the first several weeks, nearly all those that the team
cared for died anyway. They were too far gone. Gradually, though,
things began to turn around, there was food enough for everyone,
and people stopped dying.

The commissar spent a lot of time with our group and was
fascinated with the gospel. He once told them to stop talking to
him or else he might convert to Jesus. If he did so, he would lose
his career and everything it supplied him. Even then, he kept
coming back to talk. That friendship solidified our position in
Angola. Things were progressing and the future looked promising. They had no clue what was to come, but God did. He was
strengthening their faith in ways that they only understood after-
ward. He was also guiding them to prepare the people, though
they weren't fully aware of the high stakes at play.

One day as our workers were interceding for the people of
Ganda, the Holy Spirit spoke to them and told them to choose
faithful Christians and to invest in in-depth discipleship with
them. Marcia sought God and felt led to disciple Francisco, a
young leader in the body of Christ in Ganda. The other team
members each chose someone as well, and it became part of their
routine to set aside regular time to teach them. Each day team
members would travel to the village the group was discipling and

learn the Umbundo language. During this process they shared basic truths of Christian spirituality with the group, even as the group served them by teaching them the local language. Francisco and the others were growing rapidly in their faith.

Within months the team was shifting from relief work toward development. On one project they partnered with the United Nations to help the people plant more corn. The team would trade a package of household goods like a frying pan, a machete, some blankets, and some big bars of soap for a sack of corn. They would then put preservatives in the corn and store it. When the time came for planting, the sacks of corn would be given back to the people as seed. A lot of food distribution was still happening, but the people of Ganda were looking toward the future with more hope for full and productive lives.

A stunning and troubling event occurred about nine months after we began our work. UNITA rebel forces returned to Ganda and took control of the city. Our friendly commissar had to flee, and the team found themselves under the governing authority of rebels loyal to Jonas Savimbi. It looked very much like the cease-fire was crumbling. Our team stayed in Ganda and continued their work.

They didn't know it at the time, but the commissar was called to participate in a counter-attack to take back the city for the official government, with headquarters in Luanda. He was asked to fly over in a helicopter to do reconnaissance for a bombing run. Months later he told the team that as he flew over Ganda, he remembered a passage of Scripture where God spared a whole city because of one righteous man who lived there. He remembered the missionaries and thought that if God spared a city for one righteous man, shouldn't he do the same for six righteous people? This so distressed him that he began to tremble and vomit. The bombardment that would have destroyed Ganda and killed substantial numbers of people had to be called off. He had gotten the history of Sodom and Gomorrah somewhat confused, but his memory of that story, applied with power by the Holy Spirit, was good enough!

Our team labored on until February 1993. All other aid workers had left except those who served with Doctors Without Borders. Apprehension was thick in the air. What would happen next?

Then one day a UNITA officer appeared at the YWAM house. He told the team they'd have to leave town that morning. A government army column was approaching, and the rebels didn't want the YWAM team there during a battle. A plane was coming to fly them out, and they would have to leave all their belongings behind. The team asked to stay on but were refused. The officer explained that if they were harmed, it would make international news and UNITA would be blamed. Armed soldiers watched as they chose a few personal possessions, mostly photographs, as the only things they could take with them. Marcia told me she also took her chocolate.

The scene on the street was heart-rending when they left the house. News had spread swiftly, and the team's friends and many people they had discipled were gathered to say good-bye. It was a scene of mourning and desperation. The crowd wept, wailed, and lamented the team's departure. Some cried out, "They have respected us because you were here. What will happen to us now? So many of us will die."

In tears, our team could do nothing but say good-bye and head for the airport, escorted by armed soldiers. They would relocate to Benguela down on the coast and start over.

They were ushered into the plane and took off with heavy hearts. Would they ever see their friends again? How many would survive? Would the faith of those they had taught hold up in the midst of death and suffering? What would happen to those left behind?

Francisco was one of those left in Ganda. Later we found out that he was immediately arrested for having been a friend of our team. Soon the torture would start. Would faith be of any use when confronted with such overwhelmingly disastrous circumstances?

We'll see more of Francisco's story throughout this book as he faces terrible dangers armed only with his faith. I think his story will challenge, inspire, and instruct you. Meanwhile, let's look at some fascinating truths about faith.

1

Identity

I lived my childhood without any conscious desire for God or for faith. Rather, I was looking around at the world and wondering what my role and identity would be. It was a welcome challenge for me to test the things being offered and decide which of the possible roles I would play. I thought identity would come from the world around me and that it would have more to do with my function than anything else.

A dynamic, living faith was not something I expected or sought. But one night many years ago, this faith came to me, and through it God began to show me who I was, where I fit in the universe, and what my stature and nature were. This didn't come from me, and it didn't come from the world around me. It came from God, and I experienced it in my mind and heart before defining or living it. I didn't even know what was happening until later. I'm still receiving new insights about what began that night, and I am sure that I'm nowhere near total understanding. I do know that faith came to me as a gift. It was in the reality that filled me through that faith that I discovered the essence of my true identity.

I had spent that summer working on an isolated cattle ranch with my friend Danny Moody. I was fifteen. During the two months I'd been boarding with the Moody family, I had gone to church with them each Sunday as a condition of staying with them. However, they were Pentecostals, and with my Presbyterian background I understood almost nothing of what happened in their church. They used a vocabulary and had a church culture that were opaque to me.

There was another dynamic going on that I wasn't aware of at the time. In Acts 26:18 the Bible says that for us to come to God, He opens our eyes and turns us from darkness to light so that we can be forgiven and come into our inheritance. This hadn't happened with me yet. The real problem wasn't the vocabulary Danny's church used, but my spiritual blindness. Second Corinthians 3:14–16 speaks of a veil that must be taken away. God was drawing me and at the same time awaiting a sign from me that I wanted Him to take the veil away.

As the summer wore on, Dan and his family talked more and more about camp approaching and insisted that I would like it. I found it difficult to sit still through their services at church and didn't really want to go with them. Their anticipation increased as the weeks went by, though, and it seemed that my presence at camp was very important to them. I didn't want to disappoint this generous, warm-hearted family, and their enthusiasm had made me curious. When the time finally came, I went along.

When we pulled up to the campground, a large wooden tabernacle loomed, its sides silvered with years of weathering. It was a cool August night in the forest close to Eureka, California. Lots of cars were pulling in and a pall of dust hovered over the field where we parked. The original redwood trees had been cut down, and now there was a straggle of secondary growth around the simple wooden structures. In contrast to the ordinariness of the scene there was a buzz of anticipation in the air, and I couldn't help but wonder what was so special. Even so, I felt that I was probably in for yet another long testing of my patience.

When we entered the tabernacle, it looked to me like there were about two thousand people. I found a place on the end of one of the simple wooden pews. The singing was animated, but I was used to that from the Pentecostal services. This was the boredom that I had been dreading.

The speaker was a tall, lean Texan. I don't remember what he spoke about, but I can still clearly see his tan suit that glowed in the lights as he strode around the large platform. He went on in an excited manner for some time with much waving of his arms. He seemed enthusiastic, but I didn't really know why.

Then he urged non-Christians to come forward and accept Christ and be born again. I suddenly wondered if there were Hindus there. I thought I was a Christian, and it looked to me like those around me were typical Americans as well. I had no idea what being born again was, but it seemed that the speaker's appeal was safely directed to someone else, so I stayed where I was.

Then he called the Christians to the front. Danny wanted to go, so I stepped out into the aisle to let him pass. Hundreds were moving down the aisles and someone from behind bumped me forward. At that point, it was easier to just keep going rather than return to my seat, so I ended up at the front. The Texas evangelist directed us to a big prayer room behind the platform. By now I was just trying not to be different. I was embarrassed and felt like I was doing something vaguely foolish.

I noticed a low-lying shelf running the perimeter of the room. Straw mattresses had been placed underneath it, and people were kneeling on the mats to pray. I did the same, resting my elbows on the shelf. There was lots of shouting and crying going on and that's all I noticed for a while. Then I watched a spider climb the wall for a few minutes, finally concluding that I had been there a decent amount of time and that I could now get up and go. The only thing was, I hadn't said anything to God and I didn't want to be disrespectful.

It surprised me that I couldn't come up with anything to say. Our family had always gone to church and I thought I knew how to pray. I didn't, though, and no words came. I thought hard about what I could say to God as I considered my life and where I fit into the scheme of things.

My childhood had been disastrously interrupted at ten years old when my father left. I was devastated when he abandoned us. My mom went back to school at Chico State College to study for a profession and a means to support us. That meant quite limited finances and very simple living conditions. We were poor. I had been born with club feet, and a few months after my dad left, I had my third surgery. I was left substantially crippled during more than a year of recuperation, and even after that I couldn't walk or do sports with the freedom others had.

I can distinctly remember one day sitting in my bedroom and staring at the dust motes floating in a ray of sunlight streaming through my bedroom window. There wasn't much I could do outside because of the casts on my feet, so I just sat there thinking in the oppressive heat, sweat trickling down my face.

Adults were always telling me that I should study hard so that I could get a diploma. I needed the diploma so that I could get a good job. I needed a job so that I could make money. I needed money so that I could buy food to eat and have a place to live and have the clothes that I needed to be able to work. I needed to work so that I could eat. I needed to eat so that I could work. I needed to work . . .

Even at eleven years old I knew this kind of thinking was senseless. It was also my experience that as we lived out that meaningless existence, we were constantly subject to the risk of betrayal by those we most loved and depended on. I decided that life was painful and insecure, without meaning or significance. Life seemed to be a joyless struggle.

This impression of life hadn't changed from that day until my night at camp meeting four years later, though Danny's family and church friends had lives that made me think that maybe there was more potential in life than I had thought. As I knelt there that night with the smell of straw and dust in my nostrils and wondered what to say to God, I thought about those good people. I didn't have any sense that there was an answer to life hidden among them, but they were different. I decided to pray about that.

"Lord," I said, "I don't know why they're that way, but I've noticed that these people love each other more than any others I've ever known. I would like to have whatever it is that makes them that way."

That was my prayer. Looking back, it seems remarkably un-informed. It didn't have any repentance from sin. It didn't include any of the right verses from the book of Romans that I learned much later. I had no intention of being born again, nor did I even know that spiritual birth was a possibility.

I didn't expect an answer. My family's church prayer had been an exercise in expressing noble thoughts, and as far as I had been able to see, no one expected to receive answers. My intention was just to say something rhetorical that expressed respect to God and then to get out of there.

God had other ideas.

As soon as I spoke, I began to feel as if something were break-ing up inside me. I started to cry and tremble. Quiet tears now flowed freely. I was embarrassed and amazed. It felt like there was a softening going on inside me, like I was being gently but power-fully washed clean. It was very relational and loving and yet terri-ble in its power. I didn't put words to it that night, but my whole internal environment was changing. My feelings of abandonment, the cynicism that I'd built around the pain of my father's rejection, my own inadequacy, my feelings of inferiority, my embarrassment over my awkward, crippled walk, and my mother's sadness had dominated my inner landscape. Those faded away as I knelt there. They were replaced by a sense of transcendent wonder that I could not explain and that I had in no way expected.

All I knew was that I had knelt with a meaningless, hurtful life in a mundane world and returned to my feet a half hour or so later in what now appeared to be a different universe. I was surprised to see that the room had cleared out. My group was waiting for me in the cooling night air just outside the same simple, weathered building, but everything was different.

My very existence seemed to shine with promise. I felt like something wonderful might happen at any moment. I was completely convinced that my life was invested with enormous importance and meaning. This conviction was as real and solid as the ground that I was standing on, though I couldn't explain why. There was a sense of anticipation about the future welling up in me that would have been entirely foreign only minutes before. I was bewildered and overwhelmed, with no idea of what had happened, much less how to explain it to anyone.

At the same time, I had a joy that had nothing to do with my past or present circumstances. Where there had been angst, there was wonder and majesty. The universe seemed permeated with inexpressible beauty. This massive change of perspective was beyond my vocabulary to explain. I did know that it was from God, though, and that I absolutely did not want to lose it. I knew at a deep, intuitive level that I had found my place.

I was not the originator of these things. I didn't even know what was happening. I was incapable of dreaming this up, if I'd even had such an inclination. To say that something special had happened would be a massive understatement. My experience and perception of reality had shifted forever. This knowledge and this goodness came from outside myself at my invitation and filled me, permeating my whole being.

Ephesians 2:8 says, "For by grace are you saved through faith, and that not of yourselves. It is the gift of God." Faith was certainly a gift to me, as it is to everyone who will respond to God's initiative. Two verses later, Ephesians 2:10 says, "For we are His workmanship, created in Christ Jesus for good works, which God prepared beforehand that we should walk in them."

This gift of faith planted within me a certainty that I have a secure, meaningful place of belonging in the universe. God made me in His image as an individual creation. I'm not just a collection of DNA. I am an original work of God. DNA is just what He used as His tools to make that part of me that is material. I'm not just an animal who has evolved. God made me intentionally for adoption into His family.

Over the following years my understanding grew, and I came to see that I'm not to be like anyone else. I'm unique. I don't have to strive or compare myself with others. God has good works planned for me to do. I have every talent I need to do those things. He is my point of reference and the environment where I find life. He created me for adoption, full inclusion in the joy of His family (Eph. 1:4–5). I'm not alone or at loose ends. Life is meaningful and holds great promise.

On that night at the camp meeting I didn't have this biblical understanding, but I had been given faith. It was a relational gift. God had made Himself known to me, and in that knowing, faith was born. Grace had flooded into my life. I knew on a deep, inarticulate level that I was the workmanship of God. I knew that my life had a purpose. There was something substantial and significant that I was to do. Though I had no idea yet what that might be, I knew I was willing. I did know that the condition that I must fulfill to pursue all of this was to forsake evil. This glory that I experienced was purity, goodness, and love. It was utterly incompatible with impurity, selfishness, and dishonesty.

As the months went by, my Christian friends helped me find a way to express these things, and I discovered that what I had known relationally was confirmed by the written revelation from God in the Bible.

For the first time in my life, I really knew who I was. It wasn't something I had longed after before that evening in Eureka. I was vaguely unhappy with my life, but I thought that pretty much everyone was. I didn't know that the potential for a transcendent answer existed. It had never occurred to me to want it.

God wanted it for me. It is His nature to love, and He is clear about His desire that all come to know Him (Matt. 18:14; 2 Pet. 3:9). He promises to be a father to the fatherless (Ps. 68:5), and I now understand that my father's absence was another factor that moved God to look at me with special attention. He also answers prayers, and I had an uncle and aunt that were praying for me. Danny and his wonderful family and church were asking God for my salvation. When I look back, I have a mental image of God, crouched and ready, just waiting for the slightest excuse to move into my spirit and give me faith. He began that night to set things in order. It's not to my credit that I began to find my place. It was His doing (1 John 3:1–3).

However, I did have the moral obligation to respond to God that night. He didn't throw a switch and cause change in me. He appealed to me by revealing Himself. I sensed love, beauty, and purpose, and I responded with brokenness and a thirst for more. God wants love. Love cannot be caused. It must be given. I gave my love to God when He came to me. If I had wanted to resist, God would have respected my decision.

Many people develop a deep and genuine faith in God without the dramatic beginning that I experienced. They trust and obey

Him. Dramatic or not, in a life of faith there is always a witness of God's Spirit and a unifying of our spirit with His. We're born separated from God as part of a fallen race, and there is a time when He comes to us and offers faith. We respond or not to that offering from God. Multitudes don't respond and God graciously lets them go on in their own way of living. Many do respond and their spirits are united with the Spirit of God. That relational unity with God is spiritual life. They embark on a fascinating journey.

Their primary identity becomes their relationship to God as part of His family. As Paul puts it, "Because you are sons, God has sent forth the Spirit of His Son into your hearts, crying out, 'Abba, Father!' Therefore you are no longer a slave but a son, and if a son, then an heir of God through Christ" (Gal. 4:6–7; see 3:26–4:7 for context).

I didn't know this in a way that I could express yet, but there was a security and trust in me that was the evidence of the reality of what would later be understood. As we assimilate this truth, it frees us from the need for stature or for striving to impress. What relaxation can be ours!

None of us is meant to live an autonomous life, trying to avoid God's control and influence. We are meant to live in freedom, the freedom to be all that we can be when we recognize and assume our true identity as children of God. This is meant to bring us such assurance that it takes away our anxieties and frees us to really live.

This is all God's idea, and He decided on it before He created anyone (Eph. 1:4–5). This is His unalterable purpose for all of us. He will bring us in. His overwhelming generosity in making us a part of His life and family is His purpose for humanity. Nothing will change His mind. This is our identity and our assurance.

Since He is the author of my faith (Heb. 12:2), He is also the owner. I can't just make any old thing up and think that I'm the originator of my own reality. This knowing is substantive and objective reality. I didn't create it and I don't control it. I have to submit to and obey the author in order to explore it further.

What a joyous obedience it is. God is infinite in presence, in time, in knowledge, in understanding, in wisdom, and in creativity. How could there ever be a more fascinating journey than to explore the universe that His gift of faith opened to me? I'm not engaged in a dutiful, dreadful grind of moral performance, undertaken to escape hell. I'm lovingly exploring with Him the endless possibilities for love, beauty, meaning, and wonder. I'm coming out from the shadows of religious obligation to walk in the freedom that only His life in me can accomplish.

This all happens in an amazing context that exceeds my human potential. I have nothing in myself that could possibly be the source. Paul expressed this beautifully in Galatians 2:20: "I have been crucified with Christ; it is no longer I who live, but Christ lives in me; and the life which I now live in the flesh I live by faith in the Son of God, who loved me and gave Himself for me."

It is clear in Ephesians 1:4–5 that when God created humans, He was motivated by pure generosity, uncontaminated by any self-interest on His part. He didn't need us to work for Him or to continually tell Him how great He is. He didn't need us for fellowship, because He wasn't lonely. We read in John 17:20–23 about the unity and harmony of the persons of the Trinity and about their intention to include us. There was and is no flaw of any kind in the person of God. His family was and is perfect. God's nature is generous. He created us in His image to bring us into that perfection of joy and fulfillment. There was no hidden agenda. He created us for adoption (Eph. 1). Adoption is full inclusion in His family. That's where we were made to belong.

That night in Eureka I was included. God made Himself known to me. He embraced me and I became a part of His family. I was convinced of many things that I perceived but still didn't know how to express. It was real. It was transformational. It changed all of my paradigms. It was the gift of faith and the start of an entirely different way of life. My identity had been changed from a lost and abandoned boy to a child of God.

2

Power

In the 1990s I was in Macao, a region in southeastern China, visiting a team of missionaries that YWAM Brazil had sent to that city. Macao was under the governance of Portugal, much as Hong Kong was under Great Britain. The time for passing authority over to China was looming, and the city was full of mainland Chinese keeping track of everything. This created an unwillingness to do anything that might antagonize mainland authorities.

One day I was in a church service and the person beside me pointed out an elderly woman sitting off in a corner, telling me that I must introduce myself and get to know her. The woman he spoke of was dressed in simple and worn clothing and her thick glasses were taped together. She was disheveled and unremarkable. No one was paying any attention to her.

I asked my friend why I would want to know her and was told that she led the second-biggest church in Macao. I was intrigued and before we left sat down with her and a translator.

I soon discovered that the woman was mainland Chinese and had gained entrance to Macao illegally. That is why no one paid her any attention in the established churches. They were afraid to offend the Chinese government.

She had spent her life in mainland China planting churches with her husband, having recently arrived in Macao. Since she had no outlet for her ministry in Macao, she had simply started preaching in a local plaza. People flocked to hear. There didn't seem to be a human reason for this success, and I was fascinated. I asked her to tell me more of her story.

She said, "My husband and I spent our lives together planting churches. It was arduous work and we labored to the limits of our strength. When we would get very tired, the Lord would have the authorities come and arrest us. Then we would get a good rest in prison, with a lot of time to seek the Lord. When God would see that we were restored, he would have the authorities release us, and we would go back to planting new churches. This happened many times.

"The last time, though, they killed my husband and God told me that it was time for me to leave China. I came to Macao and now I'm preaching here."

There was no hint of self-pity, but rather a glow of joy and satisfaction. Here was a woman who had lived well and was deeply fulfilled. She showed no bitterness about the injustice of imprisonment and the death of her husband. She wasn't forcing a positive attitude. This grace and peace was manifestly authentic. I couldn't see any anxiety at all and wondered what earthly provision had been made for her.

I didn't want to ask her how she got into Macao, as that was sensitive information and might implicate others in illegal actions. I did ask her what she was planning to do next.

She said, "The Lord has told me that he is going to take me to America and that I will live out my days there."

She said this with such conviction and serenity that I thought that it must have already been arranged. I asked her if she had a visa. She not only didn't have a visa; she didn't have a passport, a birth certificate, or any other documents. She couldn't even show consulate officials that she was a citizen of any country.

I didn't want to discourage her, so I said nothing. I knew, though, that what she thought was going to happen was impossible. I felt sorry for her.

It was two years before I got back to Macao, but I had often thought of this woman. I had been so impressed by her buoyancy, peace, satisfaction, and strength. As soon as I saw someone who would know, I asked what had become of her. She was living in the United States!

Where does this kind of strength and power come from? Are just a few born with it or can anyone get it? What is God's plan and ambition for each of us?

How do we go from the insecurity and distance from God that characterizes most of us to the level of intimacy and faith this woman had? God made us in His image so that we would have the potential to be included through adoption. However, there is a distinct difference between the Creator and all things that are created. How could God bring unity between the two, a unity that would open the door to full inclusion?

His answer was the incarnation, and He decided on it before ever creating us (Eph. 1:4–5). In Philippians 2 the Bible shows how Jesus emptied Himself to become one of us. This is arguably the greatest act of generosity in all of eternity. Early Christian theologians who participated in the Council of Nicaea in AD 325 were fascinated by the incarnation. They wrestled with the ideas involved and distilled understanding until they came up with the Nicene Creed, used by the church to this day. They said it beautifully when they wrote that Christ is "Light from Light, true God from true God, begotten, not made." Jesus, the Son of God incarnate, was of the exact same nature as God.

At the same time He was 100 percent human. He totally iden-
tified with us by becoming one of us. His own term for Himself
was "the Son of Man." He learned from the things that He suffered
and was tempted in all ways just as we are, yet without sin. He
learned from his parents, even developing the skills of a carpenter.
When tempted, He refused divine prerogatives and dealt with the
situation as a human, though always in vital relationship with the
divine. He humbled Himself to the point of being executed as a
criminal, and took it all as a man.

In Jesus Christ we have the perfect union of the human and
the divine. In Him dwell perfect Godhood and perfect manhood.
This was such a radical concept at the time of the Nicene fathers
that they had to create a term for it. Nothing in human vocabulary
was adequate to express this. They started calling it the *hypostatic
union*. In Jesus we see a sublime blending that perfectly expresses
what God is and what man is capable of being. Hebrews 1 says that
Christ is the brightness of God's glory and the exact representation
of His person. He is also the perfect man.

He is held up to us as our example, that we might live as He
lived. In 1 Peter 2:21 we read, "To this you were called, because
Christ also suffered for us, leaving us an example, that you should
follow His steps." We can only do this if we also live with a sublime
and powerful blending of the human and the divine in us.

He is to live in us and through us. His life transforms us and
gains expression through us. Second Peter 1:3–4 says that we
receive from Him everything that we need for life and godliness
and that we can become co-participants in the divine nature. Jesus
brought into existence a wonderful union of God and man in one
being. He then offered to dwell in us through the Holy Spirit. His
life is to be our life and His nature is to be our nature. This doesn't
happen by good laws and doctrines, but only by "Christ in [us],
the hope of glory" (Col. 1:27). The life we live here on earth is a
direct result of Jesus in our hearts, blended with us in a way that

doesn't make us God but defines our true, unique identity in Him and gives us a potential beyond the merely human. His life blended with ours is the power of living by faith.

We live the supernatural reality of men and women who are no longer separated from the divine nature. God dwells in us and imparts His goodness to us. This happens through faith and it means that we are now sons and daughters of God and no longer slaves. In Galatians 4:7 it is written, "Therefore you are no longer a slave but a son, and if a son, then an heir of God through Christ."

We rightly value our forgiveness through grace, but the same grace that forgives us will do so much more. Forgiveness is just the first step. The grace giver and the grace are actually one and the same. It's the life of Christ in us that achieves growth in our expression of the divine nature through our lives. Romans 5:10 represents many Scripture passages that make this point: "For if when we were enemies we were reconciled to God through the death of His Son, much more, having been reconciled, we shall be saved by His life."

I've heard so many Christians give up on themselves and quit pursuing their dreams of intimacy with God and their desire for holiness. They sometimes exclaim, "I'm only human, after all!"

Certainly we are human, but are we only human? Doesn't the life of God fill us through the Holy Spirit? This blending of the human and the divine in our hearts is a great mystery and holds a potential beyond our comprehension. This should fill our hearts with hope, wonder, and expectation. This is who we are, and who knows what we are to become (1 John 3:2)?

Our identity is blended with His. We'll never be divine. Only God is God, and He values our humanity. However, we will never again be isolated humans, separated from Him. We're linked to the source of everything and He wants to live with us, in us, and through us. This is life and power to become children of God (John 1:12), something that religious law, codes of conduct, and ritual don't have the power to do.

Our walk within this reality is not static and it's never finished. It's a dynamic process and there is always more to learn. It's also beyond us to live out our identity if we are not in the flow of divine life, living the life of faith. God is infinite, and whatever I know of Him, there is infinitely more to learn. No matter how much He has changed me, there is more to be changed. Being born again isn't a destination as much as it is the beginning of a fascinating journey.

I am not just an heir with Christ, isolated in my individualism. My identity is wrapped up in my union with God. I am a distinct and unique individual, but I'm also more than that. The flow of my life is toward personal growth and more unity with God and with others.

Over the years, God has brought up bad things out of my heart, things that I was not previously aware of, and I've had to deal with them. I have been a disappointment to myself and to God more times than I can count. I have sinned. He has shown me new and unexpected sins in my heart even during the time that I've been writing this text. I hope that He doesn't stop, because as He uncovers my heart, I have opportunity to change and grow.

I have drifted so much in the past that I would at times find it impossible to re-create or properly remember the inner excitement of that long-ago night in Eureka, or even more recent moments of spiritual communion. The defeats come when I try to live by something other than faith.

At those times when I can't conjure up the majesty, when I can't seem to get a hold on reality, I just proceed in the conviction that everything God says in the Bible is true. I behave as if His words are true. He has said not to lie, so I don't lie. However, that is not enough. It won't produce righteousness or life.

I also need to stir myself up and seek Him, His presence, His life. Sometimes I don't feel as if I believe, but I spend time with Him. His grace flows and I obey Him. Authentic belief is the result. This authenticity doesn't come by force of will on my part. It only comes as a gift of knowing and obeying Him.

The victories come when I follow the pathways of faith. The defects in the divine-human blend that now is in me are due to me, to my deceitful heart and my lack of attention to Christ in me.

I went on to finish Bible College, marry, and become a missionary with Youth With A Mission in Brazil, where my wife and I founded the work and have now lived for over forty years. It hasn't been easy. We're engaged in a war between good and evil, and much of the opportunity to explore holistic reality with God comes in the context of struggles. We know who we are and we know whom we're fighting for. It's a great challenge—one that requires us to seek God as we wrestle for the victories that come only by faith.

3

Obedience

Our faith is inseparable from how we live our lives. Even in the first generation of Christians, there were some who wanted to lay claim to an invisible faith, a faith that existed only in their minds and that brought no evident change. James said of such an idea, "Faith without works is dead" (see James 2:14–26). In verse 18 he says that the evidence of our faith is in our works. Faith always affects and transforms how we live. It's not theory; it's reality. It's not mysticism; it's pragmatic. It's not limited to things otherworldly; it's woven into the very fabric of our lives.

If we walk by faith, we won't steal. If we walk by faith, we won't lie. If we walk by faith, we will be content with what we have, rather than coveting what others have. If we walk by faith, we will not murder. If we walk by faith, we will not commit adultery. If we walk by faith, we will put God above all else, not only in theory, but in practice. If we walk by faith, we will win great victories. If we walk by faith, we will confront apparent defeats with strong endurance. If we walk by faith, we will love those around us because God's love will be poured out in our hearts.

When we live in fellowship with God and He reveals Himself to us, great power and light come to us. We must not stop at that point, simply content to have had a moving experience. This power and light must be lived out through us. If we try to dam it up by living a life that contradicts what we see when we are communing with God, then the flow stops. You could even conclude that our experience with God then becomes destructive to us. We in our weakness cannot sustain our attempt to contain the infinite under the control of our own willfulness, even though we often try.

When we try to do this, God in His infinite and undying goodness will abort our faith to save us from destruction. In the context of our disobedience He stops the gift of faith. As James said, our faith is dead (James 2:20). Where there is no obedience, living faith is not born.

I have some friends who worked in Angola during the civil war, years after the first team had arrived there. The ministry had multiplied and branched out. One of the ways they served was to deliver supplies to a team engaged in bringing the gospel to tribes in the mountains of southern Angola. Usually three YWAMers from the larger base would be picked to do this each time. One would always be a woman so that the wife of the team leader in the tribe could have some fellowship.

All these trips were dangerous because the countryside was full of armed rebels who would rob and kill whoever they encountered. The team would establish beforehand what they would do under possible scenarios. For example, if ambushed, they would all flee to the bush, leaving the delivery pickup and supplies to guerilla fighters.

On one trip, armed men stepped into the road ahead of them. The missionaries immediately stopped their vehicle and were ready to run. However, the female team member who was with them became paralyzed with fear. She knew that she should run, but her imagination of the horrors that were about to happen was so strong that she couldn't move.

When the two men saw this, they immediately got between the woman and the bandits, hoping this would help her escape. As they walked down the dirt road, hands in the air, giving themselves up to the mercy of men who had no mercy, she was able to flee.

The two men were captured. The leader of the group commanded them to show what they had in the pickup. After bandits had examined everything, the fatal command was given. The two missionaries were told to take their shirts off and lie facedown on the ground. They knew that this was a death sentence. The shirt is taken off because the guerillas want to use it and don't want it all messed up with blood and brain matter. The order to lie facedown is because the easiest way to kill someone is to shoot him in the back of the head.

Our two young missionaries, one a Brazilian and one an Angolan, did as they were told. They knew they were going to die. The Brazilian was a husband and father of a baby boy, and all he could think of was that he would never see his wife and son again.

The Angolan, as he was preparing to lie down, said to their executioners, "We are followers of Jesus, and we want you to know that we forgive you for what you are about to do." Then he lay down, face to the ground, awaiting the fatal shot. He heard the action of the AK-47 when it was pulled back, jacking a round into the firing chamber. Then, from over by the pickup came the voice of the commander, "Let them go. No one is going to die here today." The two men jumped up and ran into the bush. The fighters took all the supplies but left the pickup. The two missionaries found their team member who had fled and they sped back to the base.

But the story was not over. The team in the mountains still needed supplies.

Later I was talking to the Brazilian who had been driving that day. He told me, "During the robbery I was okay. Later, though, I shook uncontrollably as I imagined what had almost happened to us." He went on to tell me, "It took three days before I was willing to go back down that road again, taking supplies to the team."

We had a clear responsibility to supply that team. This worker knew that he was the one who had to do it. It was clear to him that this was what God wanted. Would he obey in the face of such emotional trauma and overwhelming danger? He obeyed the Lord. They took the supplies to the team.

His faith lived and grew. It wasn't aborted. It wasn't dead. He obeyed.

This is an extreme example, but the principle applies to the mundane details of our daily lives. When we disobey, our faith is damaged and will die. When we obey, our faith lives and impels us toward more faith and obedience.

When I was a junior in high school, my school counselor called me to a meeting in his office. He wanted to know what I was going to do with my life. I was at a point of gaining confidence that God wanted me to be a missionary. The only way I knew to pursue that was to go to Bible college.

I knew, though, that this wasn't what the counselor would want to hear, so when he asked me what I was going to do, I mumbled, almost inaudibly, that I was going to go to Bible college and be a missionary. He didn't hear me, so I had to repeat it a little more clearly.

He didn't like my answer. I had gotten very good scores on standardized college entrance tests. That, together with my grades in high school and the modest means of our family, had resulted in my getting a full scholarship from the State of California as well as a federal grant. Those would cover my expenses to study at any university in California. The doors had opened for me to study whatever I wanted at whatever university I preferred. This could have led to a life of success, recognition, money, and privilege.

My counselor told me that I was throwing all of that away. He wanted what was best for me, so he tried to talk me out of it. That first meeting didn't last long, because he was flummoxed by my decision and he didn't know what to do.

Two weeks later he called me back to his office. He had prepared his argument carefully, even by finding a Christian group that believed that no one should be in full-time ministry on the basis of the verse in the Bible that says that everyone should work with their own hands. He did his earnest best to help me. From his perspective on life and opportunity, a perspective that didn't include faith, I was throwing my life away. He tried to convince me to go to a university of high reputation and study to be a research scientist.

This was confusing to me. I could see that he was trying to help, but I couldn't see how to do what he was proposing. What loomed large for me was the will of God. The more I was counseled to live for my own desires, the more I became convinced that God really did want me to be a missionary. I wanted the security, recognition, and income that the counselor was describing but would have to turn my back on obedience to God in order to have them. I couldn't do that to God after He had revealed Himself to me. He had made Himself known, and I knew. Now I had to obey.

I didn't know the Scriptures very well yet, but I was sensing on a spiritual level that to deny God obedience was to deny Him love.

In John 14:15–16 Jesus says, "If you love Me, keep My commandments. And I will pray the Father, and He will give you another Helper, that He may abide with you forever." The nature of faith is the dynamic of our living relationship with God. Here Jesus promises the Holy Spirit, but this promise is to those who obey. It's down-to-earth. It's pragmatic. It's relational. It doesn't admit to justifying abstractions or mystical sleight of hand.

Jesus returns to this theme two more times in this chapter, in verses 21 and 23–24. The whole development of our faith—that is, the advance of the depth and power of our relational knowledge of God—is inextricably bound up with our response of obedience to what He wants us to do.

This certainly includes what is written in the Scriptures. It also includes Jesus leading us in steps of detailed obedience as He guides our lives and reveals His very personal will to each one of us. The disciples had to leave everything and follow Him when He spoke to them. Without that obedience there would have been no living faith.

I encourage you to think of faith relationally, rather than thinking of it in a legal or transactional sense. What does it mean relationally when we fail to obey the Lord?

It might mean that we don't trust that God really loves us and has our good in mind. Because we distrust Him, we won't participate with Him in doing His will. We withhold our obedience because we think that we can trust only ourselves. This is an insult to God and destructive of our relationship to Him. But if we will express to Him our desire to trust Him, He will graciously work with us to establish this trust in us.

It might mean that we know that He loves us and has good intentions in His dealings with us. We also know that He is the source of all wisdom and knows much better than we could what is best. However, we have desires. These are immediate and gratifying. All things considered, we decide to pursue our desires, even though we might be conscious that this is not the best for God or for us. There might be some vague thought that someday we will make things right, after we have enjoyed ourselves. The result is that we don't follow Him in obedience. He has made Himself known, but the reality of that wonder fades with our disobedience. In the end, we are far from Him and confused.

I suspect that this last scenario is the most common. We violate the love He offers us for the sake of what we want. Our faith is deadened. He withdraws and patiently waits for us to turn to Him in obedience so that He can again begin making Himself known and renew the life of faith in us.

God is presented in Isaiah 45:15 as the God who hides Himself. In places like Proverbs 8:17 and Jeremiah 29:13 He promises to be found, but only by those who seek Him with all their heart. Even in 2 Corinthians 3:16–18, where there is a wonderful promise of having the veil taken away so we can see the Lord, we only see Him as though in a mirror. This limited view is means for powerful transformation. In 1 John 3:2 we are tantalized with the wondrous promise of something beyond our current state as children of God. We shall be like Him. The secret of this transformation, of becoming like Him, is in seeing Him as He is.

Why is God reluctant to reveal all to us? Why does He demand that we seek Him with all our hearts if we are to find Him? Why does He make no such promise to casual inquirers? I'm sure there are many more layers of understanding in this area, but here's one perspective that might help us begin.

In Luke 12:48 Jesus says, "For everyone to whom much is given, from him much will be required; and to whom much has been committed, of him they will ask the more." In James 3:1 we read that some teachers will receive a stricter judgment. What is the Lord showing us here?

Light is equal to responsibility. God doesn't require of us that which we don't know. In the Luke passage, we see that those who do things worthy of stripes (punishment) but without knowledge will receive fewer stripes than those who disobey in rebellion against what God has already shown them. The more we know, the more we are responsible for. When that knowledge comes through direct experience in the presence of the Lord, when it comes from Him making Himself known to us, the violation of that light is a grievous violation of His offering of the unimaginable gift of intimacy with Him.

If the Lord sees that we are not walking in the things that He has already shown us, He becomes to us the God that hides Himself.

He waits. He waits for obedience. He waits for our faith to live. He knows that if He shows us more, we will not obey the new when we haven't obeyed the old. Our relationship with God isn't so much a matter of how much we know as it is a matter of how much we walk in obedience to what He has shown us. It's not where we are on the spectrum between sinfulness and holiness, but what direction we are going and how well we are caring for our friendship and intimacy with Him. If we stay close, He will get us there.

When Pam, my wife, was a free-spirited teenager in Hawaii, she took a temporary job at a circus during spring break. There she was befriended by another circus employee. When the ten-day run was over, he asked her for a ride to the airport. He was from another country, had been robbed in the US, and had taken the circus job to get money to get back home. He didn't have a car. Pam agreed to take him to the airport.

After he checked in, he asked Pam if they could talk before he boarded the plane. They sat down on a bench in the Honolulu International Airport, and he shared with Pam how he had been a criminal in his home country and ended up in jail. While he was there, a young man told him about Jesus. He embraced the light, was born again, and his life was transformed.

He asked if Pam wanted Jesus. She knew that this was the answer for her life and said yes. He prayed with her, and her heart was filled.

The final call for his flight rang overhead. Pam's friend hurriedly reached into his carry-on and pulled out a booklet, the Gospel of John.

"Here, read this every day and pray and you will be fine," he said as he gave it to her.

Then he ran for his plane. Pam never saw him again, but things had radically changed inside of her. She would read chapter 1 of John and understand nothing; however, her heart would warm to the sacred words. Her life changed dramatically. She now knew things from God that she couldn't understand in the text. Her friends didn't hang out with her anymore because darkness and light don't mix well. She didn't know if there were any others like the man in the airport, but she was going to walk with Jesus.

About a month after Pam's rebirth, there was a chapel service at her private high school. Not being a Christian school, chapel could be almost anything. That day, though, there was a young man named Tom Raimey. He preached the gospel with authenticity and power. Pam's spirit recognized that here was someone with a message like the man at the airport. As soon as he finished, she ran up to him.

With urgency she asked, "What are you?"

He said, "Well, I'm a Christian, but why do you ask?"

"Whatever you are, that's what I am, but I don't know what I am. I have to find out what you are so I will know what I am."

"Well, I'm a Christian."

"Do you Christians have churches?" she asked.

It turned out that his church was on the other side of Oahu, close to where she lived. When Sunday morning came around, it was a beautiful day so she went to the beach. At 10:45 a.m. she stood up, shook the sand out of her mat, and rolled it up. She took an oversized T-shirt out of her bag and put it on over her bikini, slipped flip-flops on her feet, and headed for the Sunday morning service at the local Assembly of God church!

She knew nothing about church life and culture. She knew little about Jesus and the Bible. She probably didn't make a very good impression at the church that morning, but she was lovingly received and found her spiritual home.

By any external measure she wouldn't have been among those who would be judged to be the most spiritual in that Sunday morning service, but she was walking in all the light that she knew. She had obeyed the little she knew. God could trust her to obey what He showed her, and He began to show her a lot.

Other people in that service were probably very experienced and knowledgeable about the Bible and the Christian life. They would have looked much more impressive than Pam on that morning. God, though, doesn't look at the outside. In John 7:24 Jesus advises us, "Do not judge according to appearance, but judge with righteous judgment." He sees things that we don't.

We are to take care of our relationship with Him. We should facilitate Him making Himself known to us in every way that we can, not least through obedience to what He has revealed to us.

This seems to be a matter not of cold obedience to principle but of a living obedience that results from an encounter with God. In 1 John the Holy Spirit makes great promises of victory in our lives (e.g., 1:7; 2:5, 28–29; 4:7–16; 5:4). This victory, though, is predicated on being born again. It's always knowing God and then having victory. It's never obedience to concepts in order to gain acceptance and intimacy.

John Wesley was a dedicated young Christian. He was disciplined and methodical in his pursuit of a life that measured up to moral demands and codes of conduct. In this fervor and dedication he traveled from England to North America as a missionary to Native Americans. His efforts met with a lack of success, though, so he decided to return to England, defeated.

On the trip, the small sailing vessel carrying Wesley was overtaken by a terrible storm. Everyone on board was despairing and in a state of anxiety and panic. John Wesley was no different.

However, there was one group that sat on deck and sang hymns to the Lord. They were a group of Moravians. They evidenced great peace and rest in their souls. They weren't faking it to impress. What would be the point? This was authentic and impressive to Wesley.

In the end, the ship didn't sink and all aboard made it to England.

Wesley couldn't get the group of Moravians out of his mind. They obviously had some source of power, peace, grace, and joy that he didn't. Now he was dissatisfied with his Christianity and began to seek more. One night he felt his "heart strangely warmed," as he recorded in his diary, and God made Himself known.

From that time on, John Wesley's ministry evidenced great power. His life had an impact that changed the conscience of England and even changed the world. Out of his spiritual vitality, movements were born that changed laws, abolished slavery, and influenced nations as diverse as India and New Zealand.

This was no ordinary life, but Wesley didn't do all of this through his abilities or through his dedication. He had those when he failed in North America. The power came when God arrived with the gift of faith, making Himself known. Then Wesley's discipline and dedication became wonderful receptors for God's ongoing revelation of Himself, the ongoing gift of faith. Wesley followed the Lord with extraordinary attention, but the power and virtue came from God.

Francisco, Part 2

After the team of missionaries left Ganda, which had been taken over by UNITA rebel forces, they had no way to communicate with the people there. Francisco passed out of sight and hearing but not out of mind. They prayed much for him and for the others.

Two years later, down on the coast in Benguela, the team was preaching the gospel and feeding those who had fled the war. They had helped build large tent cities for refugees and had set up a network of church volunteers. At the program's height, more than thirty thousand people were being fed at ninety-eight feeding centers. Discipleship training programs had also been started, and we had our first Angolan missionaries. I was in town visiting the team and ministering to them.

As soon as I began to speak to the group on the first day, I noticed a well-dressed woman among them who didn't look like one of our YWAMers. After class they introduced me. She was the local army general's wife. A day or two later she brought her husband back to meet us.

The general wanted to have a Brazilian barbecue, a churrasco, as a way of celebrating my visit. Our guys told him that the meat available in the local market would be too tough to eat if we roasted it over coals. He was determined, though, and sent a helicopter to Namibia to get a tender young steer.

That put me on the spot. I had to explain to him that despite his efforts, I wouldn't be able to go to the churrasco. I had to catch a flight to the island nation of São Tomé and Príncipe from Luanda, Angola, on Monday. The last flight to Luanda was on Saturday, the day of the churrasco. The general promised to arrange a plane for me on Sunday, so I stayed.

It was a good day at the general's big white mansion on the hill. We had a great barbecue and hours of interesting conversation. He seemed to have a sincere heart of concern for the well-being of his people. He had also recently been through a close call when he was shot in the chest during a battle. He'd narrowly escaped with his life, and this had created some fears and some questions in his mind and heart. At the end of the afternoon we prayed with him, though he wasn't a believer like his wife. He seemed moved by whatever God did in him during the prayer. Then evening arrived, and we left the general's home.

When we arrived back at the YWAM house, a colleague told me that Francisco had arrived from Ganda. He was in the backyard and he wanted to talk to me. I went immediately and we greeted one another. He pulled up three tiny stools, and we squatted in the darkness with his nephew, Paulino. I asked Francisco what had happened to him after our team left Ganda. He smiled in the hot darkness, waving his hand around his face to get relief from the mosquitoes, and told me his story.

Almost as soon as our team departed, UNITA officials had arrested Francisco. They assumed our team had a two-way radio to communicate with the outside world, but when they went through the team's possessions, it was nowhere to be found. Because Francisco was known to be a friend to the YWAMers, the police decided that he must have the radio, or at least know where it was hidden.

For two weeks they beat and tortured Francisco for information about the radio. They went to his house and ruined it, digging through the floor and walls to see if it had been hidden. I think Francisco would have told them where it was if it indeed had existed, but there was no radio. Our team had never had one.

When it became clear that they wouldn't get anything out of Francisco regarding the radio, rebel officers changed their approach. Now they told Francisco that since he was a leader in the community and the government hadn't killed or imprisoned him, they could only believe that he was a government agent. They left him in jail.

One day they came and told him that if he would kill for them, they would believe he was on their side and not a government spy. They had people they wanted dead and offered Francisco an AK-47 to kill them. If he killed for them, he would live. If he refused to kill for them, he would die.

This seemed like an impossible situation. On the one hand was certain death. On the other hand was terrible transgression and violence. Where could Francisco get the grace to strengthen his faith, refuse to kill, and trust in God through obedience?

4

Reality

Hebrews 11:1 says, "Now faith is the substance of things hoped for, the evidence of things not seen." I had an encounter with substance and evidence that night in Eureka. It wasn't material, but it did have substance. It wasn't perceptible by my five senses, but it was conclusive evidence for experiencing God. He came to me in relationship; therefore I can live and hope and begin to understand what's really important.

This wasn't true because I believed it. I saw and responded to the Truth, the person of Jesus. I couldn't say, "I believe in this so it is true for me." It didn't originate with me. My believing it or not would make no difference as to its reality. It is true and defines the nature of reality, both for those who believe and for those who won't believe.

I didn't find out who I was by looking inside. It is impossible to be my own source of truth on this journey. Without an outside point of reference, all of us are lost. Every ship on the seas needs a navigational system. Earlier navigators used the stars. Ships today can use satellites. There has to be an outside reference point.

In our postmodern world, many like to pick and choose their gods. Spiritual truth is often seen as something that is manufactured by each individual, with no objective reality. Hence, I think that I can make my god or gods according to my needs and preferences. In this worldview, I believe in spirituality, but there are no unchangeable truths. It's all sourced out of my preferences and completely subjective. Your god is one way, mine is another, and we're all good with that. Let's say that someone prefers the spirituality of vampires, witches, and warlocks. From this point of view, that's up to them and shouldn't be seen as right or wrong, as good or evil.

Is this way of seeing things aligned with reality? Is God someone we discover, or is He someone we make up?

When I was a small boy, there was a trout lake about fifteen miles from our home in northern California, its crystalline waters set in beautiful pine forests. My dad kept an old wooden boat there and occasionally we would go to fish. This was a heavy craft and we didn't have a motor. The boat had oarlocks and my dad would row us around as we fished. Every time I asked my dad if I could row, but he always told me that I was too small. Then one day when I was seven or eight years old, he said I could try.

I sat on the bench seat in the early evening of that bright, sunny day and watched as my dad placed the oars in their locks and put handles in my hands. Off we went—sort of. Try as I might, I couldn't keep to any kind of course. I was rowing in circles. It didn't matter how careful I stroked the oars, I just couldn't hold a course. My dad watched and kept his silence. I was getting more and more frustrated. Finally I looked up at him and asked, "How do I do this?" Then he taught me.

He asked where I wanted to go, and I pointed across the lake to a good fishing spot. He had me maneuver the boat around until its bow was pointed at that spot. Of course, my back was toward the prow, and when positioned to row, I couldn't see where we were headed. My dad had me look back and asked me to find a distant landmark. I chose an old snag that had been hit by lightning. It stood white and skeletal against the green of the pine forest.

"Now," my dad said, "keep that snag directly behind the boat."

I did, making little corrections between the bigger strokes. We soon got to the place where we wanted to fish, and I got to feel good about my little accomplishment.

We all need an outside reference point. We need help. If we expect to find our own truth that will somehow come mysteriously out of somewhere inside us, we will only row in circles and our journey won't take us anywhere.

God is not only the author of my faith but also the finisher (Heb. 12:2). I can't make my faith up, and I won't grow my faith by a direct effort to do so. I need to seek God, and He will grow my faith. The answers aren't in me; they're in Him. I'm pursuing. That pursuit is based on His input. It doesn't come out of my own heart. The initiation comes from Him, not from me.

It seems obvious to me that "I have experienced Him who is the source of all reality, therefore I know" is a much better epistemology, a much better starting place for life and understanding, than the "I think, therefore I am" of French philosopher René Descartes. There was no "leap of faith" here for me. I didn't make up something because I needed it. I didn't just choose to believe in a rosy theory of reality because I preferred it. I didn't generate something out of a determined practice of positive thinking. God came to me and made it impossible for me to continue to be honest and at the same time deny faith in His reality. He initiated this journey of faith. It's been going on for forty-five years and is more radical and compelling now than ever before.

God is the source of life. That life becomes light for us (John 1:4). Physical light gives form and reveals material reality to us. The Lord's life in us completes our knowledge, as it unfolds for us the form and shape of invisible, spiritual reality and rounds out our understanding of the nature of things. He is the fountain of life, and that life lights our perceptions (Ps. 36:9).

I haven't always maintained a closeness to God. During my early twenties I had some devastating relational failures, and the pain and disappointment were so deep that I decided not to walk with God anymore. I drew close to friends who also didn't believe, and I went about establishing a life that didn't include God.

One day a couple of months into this miserable effort to abandon reality, I was playing chess with my neighbor. There was a news piece about the "Jesus People" movement on the television in the background. I made some disparaging remark about Christians.

He looked at me and said, "But you are a believer. Don't you believe in Jesus?"

I opened my mouth to deny it and found that I couldn't. It would have been such a violation of what I truly knew that I couldn't bring myself to be that hypocritical.

My frustration and feelings of desolation were so great that I wanted to pretend I didn't know. Maybe I wanted to get back at God for my troubles. Maybe I'd lost hope in being able to live as God wanted me to. Maybe I just wanted to leave behind the whole area of spirituality, feeling that I had been a dismal failure at it.

When the moment with my neighbor came, though, I couldn't deny that I did believe in Jesus as the Bible reveals Him and as I had experienced Him. Later that same day I was lying on my bed, thinking. Where did I think I could go to get away from God? How dense could I be? I sighed and told Him that I wouldn't try to deny the faith that He had given me anymore. I hadn't been responding to it, but it was there in the background and it wouldn't leave me. I gave up my resistance to Him and have never returned to that pathetic attempt to deny reality, to live a life of unbelief.

It's not only my personal experience that convinces me. I've seen over and over that we start knowing about the truly important issues of life when we're given this gift of faith. The light comes on, as I saw it happen for a woman in Brazil.

I'm usually happily occupied and my calendar is normally full. Each speaking invitation presents me with decisions on how to best use my time. After much prayer and vacillation I had finally agreed to be the speaker at a missions conference in Londrina, a city of four hundred thousand in the South of Brazil. When the day arrived, I flew down with a small team of fellow missionaries. The friend who had invited me was waiting at the airport to pick us up. It was good to see him, but his expectation for the conference seemed quite different from the optimism he had shown during the invitation process.

"Jim," he said, "we have never done this sort of event before, and we don't know if anyone will come. You speak to the pastors tomorrow morning. If they like what you say, we could have a reasonable audience in the evening service."

I wasn't thrilled by his pessimism. It had been hard for me to leave my family and to get away from a busy schedule, and the last thing I wanted was to spend five days doing something that would have no impact. Our little team settled into an apartment downtown and we prayed a lot.

I spoke to the pastors the next morning, and they must have liked something. The first night we had six hundred in attendance. My friend was very pleased. It was more than he had expected. Our best hopes were already being met.

God was doing something beyond our expectations that week. The second night we had a thousand attending. The third night the crowd couldn't fit into the twelve-hundred-seat theater where we were holding the event. News had been getting around town, and a local television crew came to film a report.

These things don't generally happen at mission conferences! After all, we weren't doing a divine healing campaign or promising prosperity. We were challenging people to make personal sacrifices in order to reach those who had never heard the gospel.

This was something that transcended our program. One woman came to me on the third day and profusely thanked me for the salvation of her husband. It seems that he had been resisting the gospel for twenty years but had completely given his life to the Lord the night before, when I had talked about money. I asked her how that had led to her husband's conversion, and she had no answer. God was doing things beyond what we had planned. I even had two other people come to me outside the context of the meetings and ask how they could know God. That's unusual!

By the fourth night we had to move to another venue, a big gymnasium, and about three thousand people came. God's manifest presence was strong that night and everyone seemed aware of it. The acoustics were terrible, though, and by the time I finished speaking, I was tired. As soon as I could break free, I headed across the basketball court, attempting to make my getaway. I had only gone about thirty feet when I saw one of the sponsoring pastors striding in my direction, pulling a young woman along by her left arm, with a young man holding her other one.

"Jim," the pastor said, "this woman is his wife." He pointed his chin at the young man. "He was unfaithful to her as an unbeliever, but now he has been saved for six months. She won't trust him. We want you to pray that her attitude will change."

While the pastor was speaking, the woman didn't even look up. Her head was downcast and her lustrous, dark hair was hanging down, making it impossible to see her face. She was leaning back against the pull of the pastor's grasp. I felt sorry for her. It seemed reasonable and maybe even wise to me that she would hesitate in trusting her husband for a time. I wanted to be kind to her, though, and decided that it would be quicker to just pray than to debate this with the pastor.

I put my hand on her shoulder and began to pray all sorts of blessing on her life. My heart had gone out to her, and the prayer came from the Spirit. Suddenly she began to shake. I peeked from under my partially closed eyelids and saw her throw her hair back and look at me with startled intensity. She was crying. Suddenly she grabbed me in a tight hug. I just kept praying while her husband and his pastor watched. When I finished, they led her away, still crying. I knew that something serious had happened, but there was no explanation because she was crying too hard to talk.

The next and final night, we had what looked to be about five thousand people in attendance. After the message there was a line of people wanting prayer, and I was attending to each one. Suddenly the woman from the night before came striding across the gymnasium, pulling her husband by the arm.

She came straight up to me and with a penetrating look asked, "What was that?"

"I don't know," I said. "What do you mean?"

"Last night it was no longer just you praying," she explained. "Suddenly it was like a bright, white light was penetrating to the depths of my spirit. I have never been so scared and I have never been so full of joy. I have never felt anything so frightening and I have never experienced anything so sublime. I went home crying. I went to bed crying. I got up this morning crying. But it wasn't because I was sad. It was this wonderful presence with me. I don't want to lose it. I have to know what it is."

I gave the best explanation I could in the limited time available and referred her to her husband's pastor.

The light had gone on for that woman. She was experiencing faith. She was experiencing God. To experience faith and to experience God is the same thing. I especially like this story because I didn't tell her what to expect. The whole situation was so embarrassing for her that I just wanted to pray quickly and let her go. God did something that neither she nor I expected. It was spontaneous and genuine for her, and she gave me one of the most beautiful descriptions of a first encounter with God that I have ever heard.

She had no idea what doctrines she believed in. She wasn't even interested in acquiring doctrines, but she knew that God was real.

He had given her faith. He had given her Himself. The hurt with her husband was pushed completely into the background. This new light was now her primary reality.

This light is the starting point for understanding all the truly important things about life. It comes from God and doesn't fit into a materialistic, proof-based epistemology.

Many people today start by demanding scientific evidence for everything. The trouble is, science has a limited scope of authority. The scientific method is good at helping us grow in our understanding of material reality. If you want to know how gravity works, ask a scientist. Scientists don't understand everything about it, but they will be able to talk about some interesting facts and possibilities. Where cause and effect over material substance is the question, science gives the best answers we're capable of. This has enabled humanity to make great progress in technology, but to what end?

If you are a materialist, no matter how sophisticated your words and intricate your reasoning, you either exercise great care to maintain a lack of definition, or you eventually get to the same place I stumbled upon as an eleven-year-old. There's no meaning or significance. We have physical knowledge of the world today like never before in history, but that doesn't make life worth living, nor does it tell us how to use all the technology.

Why am I here? What should I be doing? Where am I going? People who have invested their faith in the ideas of the Enlightenment (the Age of Reason) often disparage these inquiries, possibly because science can't really say anything about them. They are beyond the competence of science's limited authority. To decide that nothing more than the material exists, not only goes against millennia of human experience, but is also nothing more than an assertion. It is a made-up conviction, and one could be forgiven for suspecting that it might be motivated by a deep desire to escape from God's perceived demands. It's not evidence, and its only substance is denial of what has not been proven. That denial is based on nothing more substantial than emotional prejudice that grows out of all kinds of complex motivational foundations.

Jesus attributes moral significance to belief. He doesn't emphasize meticulous observance of detailed regulations. Rather, we set the tone of our moral posture by responding or not responding to God's initiative. When He comes to us, His goodness can be clearly experienced, even if it's only vaguely understood. We know experientially that He is incompatible with anything that is destructive, hurts others, betrays trust, or damages relationships. We sense and know that to accept what God offers we must give that up. We can't generate faith. We can't be the origin of this gift, but we can embrace it. In that embracing we automatically and instinctively commit ourselves to living out His goodness. If we will do that for Him, our journey begins.

Today many want to make up a mixture of beliefs. They set out to generate a context for their lives out of an obscure blending of desires and impulses that not even they clearly understand (Jer. 17:9–10). This patchwork faith of personal preference reveals a great deal about the individual that creates it, but it tells us virtually nothing about reality.

Jesus is not making anything up. He's grounded in reality that is infinitely older than the material universe. On this journey, He's not counting how many times we fail but watching whether we're continuing our journey of faith with honesty. Faith gives us the strength and security necessary to be done with pretending. It dispenses with the need to protect ourselves through masks of hypocrisy. When He who is absolute glory and greatness has adopted and filled you, it is no longer important to impress anyone. He is your security and your identity.

Unbelief can have honest intellectual questions tangled with its emotional urges. However, its essence seems to be either a matter of the timing of God's faith initiative in that life or an active refusal of honest relational interaction with Him. We don't want Him telling us what we should do. I've lived both the intellectual problems and the emotional refusal to submit, and they are both miserable.

It's true that there are many ways to deal with life that don't include biblical faith, but they just substitute hope in reason or science or one's own preferences or an unbiblical god or animistic spirits or something else for the hope that can be found in Him. Only the hope that is a result of the faith that comes in an encounter with God unites us with foundational reality that is older than the stars and as new as your next spiritual discovery.

Hebrews 11:3 says, "By faith we understand that the worlds were framed by the word of God, so that the things which are seen were not made of things which are visible" (see also 1 John 2:24–27). If we go back far enough, there was no stuff. There were no stars or planets or rocks or trees. There were no molecules. There was not even a lowly quark. Then, suddenly, there was a lot of material substance, a lot of stuff.

What happened? Was there anything before there was material reality? Hebrews 11, as well as many other Scriptures, clearly states that there was a reality before the material world came into being. This reality also has substance, just not material substance.

Once a woman with a chronic illness sought out Jesus for healing (Luke 8:43–48). She thought that if she could just touch the hem of his clothing, she would be healed. She pushed through a crowd and managed to touch his garment. She was healed.

Jesus's reaction is interesting and informative. He asked who had touched him. The disciples were confused because so many people were pressing in on them that many were jostling Jesus. He said, "Somebody touched Me, for I perceived power going out from Me" (Luke 8:46). Something moved. It went from inside Jesus to outside. He could feel it.

This wasn't material substance, but it was substantial. It was spiritual substance, just as real as physical substance but not material and therefore not subject to physical examination. The woman

I met in Londrina knows about this. So do I, and so do the billion or so other people around the world who have Jesus in their hearts. A thing doesn't have to be material to be real.

In the beginning, there was personality and there was spirit. A universe existed that didn't have stars, planets, or anything material. It was made up of the person of God in the substance of spirit. Then the physical happened. It happened when God spoke. It was the Word of God that framed the worlds and created them. All material reality is really just the Word of God secondhand!

A life of faith that is both the evidence of and the expression of our relationship with God is a life founded on the bedrock of reality. Anything else is less real, less satisfying, and less enduring.

5

Transformation

I have tried on many occasions to generate faith by positive think-ing. Like everyone else who has experimented with this, I have not been successful. It's been a relief to discover that Scripture doesn't teach that faith is a strong conviction that we can generate out of ourselves or maintain by carefully controlling our attitudes.

I mentioned that I was born clubfooted, and I have always wanted to have normal, healthy feet. After my first encounter with God at the camp meeting in Eureka, I would go forward in church at every opportunity to receive prayer for healing. On several occa-sions the preacher who prayed for me would explain that I hadn't been healed because I lacked faith. If I only had faith, he would say, I would be healed.

This made me feel that I had failed. Not only was I without healing, but also it seemed that God must be disappointed in me. Jesus's greatest moments of disappointment with the disciples came because of their unbelief, and I wasn't believing. He was kept from changing much or doing a miracle because of my pitiful faith. He wasn't getting honored, and I wasn't getting healed.

It got to the point that I would go forward thinking over and over again as fast as I could, "I believe. I believe. I believe." There was always a little echo at the back of my mind that said, "No you don't," in between every "I believe." I had a general faith in God, but I had no faith in my faith. It just went nowhere.

Then one day several years later, soon after I entered YWAM, I was in Mexico. I was visiting some teams that had come together after a summer of evangelization in Central America. We were having a prayer meeting one morning when one of the women doubled over and collapsed against the girl beside her. The woman who had collapsed began to whisper something in the girl's ear, and when the girl heard it, she began to weep. Then she asked for attention from the whole group and began to explain.

Three months earlier the sick woman had gotten a diagnosis of cancer that had spread through her lymph system. She had only a few months left to live. She decided that she wanted to spend that time serving God, so she sold her house and joined YWAM. She didn't mention the illness on her application forms because she was afraid that she would be turned down. She was accepted and came to the outreach.

During the summer she'd had a period of three days when she was extremely ill and in pain. She didn't know who or where she was. After those three days, her health and understanding returned to a more normal state, and the team moved on. Still she told no one about the cancer, and no one in YWAM knew what was going on.

Now during our prayer meeting, the pain was spiking again and she thought she was dying. She explained her disease and asked for prayer.

The group responded with spontaneity and intensity out of the closeness of the shared struggles of the summer. Everyone prayed with focus and genuine emotion, and most were loud. Suddenly, in the middle of it all, I knew that the woman had been healed. The presence of God was powerful. The unity among the group was as near to perfect as I had ever seen. The intensity was whole-hearted. Something in that whole mix just reached a point that the Spirit witnessed with me that she was healed. The moment after I received that conviction, someone read Psalm 91 out loud: "A thousand may fall at your side, / And ten thousand at your right hand; / But it shall not come near you . . ."

The sick woman stood up, announcing that her pain was gone. She was well. Later tests with doctors in the States confirmed that her cancer was gone.

I began to get the first glimmerings of understanding. I have seen such answers to pray more than a few times since. There is a pattern, not of attaining an acceptable standard in my attitude, but of the gift of the confirmation of the Spirit before or at the time of seeing the answer. The conviction of an answer comes from God, not from bare human insistence.

My faith was growing as Pam and I got married, and within a year of our wedding I stepped out in the obedience of faith and went to Brazil. It wasn't positive thinking, though. It was more of God and His grace, and that grace established us in that new context.

About a decade after we moved to Brazil, I was in the high Andes Mountains of southern Peru for a regional leaders' meeting. We spent a week seeking God, learning from one another, making decisions, and strengthening our unity.

The leader of YWAM in Canada had brought an eighty-year-old Episcopalian pastor named Bob with him. We were in the Sacred Valley of the Incas at twelve thousand feet altitude. The air was thin, and I wondered if it was wise to bring a man of that age to such a place. He seemed to do fine, but some of us were a bit worried.

There was going to be an outreach in Cuzco, once the capital of the Inca Empire, starting on the Monday following our leaders' meetings, but we had the weekend off. Those of us from Brazil had decided that we would catch a train down to Machu Picchu, a well-preserved ruin from the Inca Empire.

The Canadian director asked if I would look after Pastor Bob, who wanted to go with us. I hadn't counted on this, but how could I refuse? I just hoped that he would be all right. Little did I know how much of a surprise was awaiting me.

We rose from sleep in the predawn darkness and cold of the Andes to catch our shuttle bus down to the train station. Our group of six Brazilians was mussed and rumpled, with sleep heavy on our faces. Pastor Bob wasn't there, and I thought hopefully that maybe he had decided not to go. Then, just before the shuttle bus was to leave, he appeared. He was wide awake, serene, and well groomed. His Bible was tucked under his arm. He had been out praying!

The train station was chaotic, and at one point I lost sight of Pastor Bob. The calm and spacious tourist train was there at the time, and he had gotten on. It was too expensive for us, so we got him off, just in time. Then the local train came.

This train was old and crowded. People were getting on with their belongings tied up in bundles, and some had chickens or goats. There was no place to sit, and I was worried about Pastor Bob. As the train chugged slowly toward our destination, women came up and down the aisles selling roasted goat meat, boiled manioc root, and other snacks. Conversation was animated and loud. Bob looked just as serene as he had before dawn. At last, after four hours of standing, we were able to get him a seat.

We disembarked at the small mountain town called Aguas Calientes. As the train pulled away, we stood beside the tracks and enjoyed the exotic setting. The mountains rose almost straight up on all sides. This seemed as close as one can get to the end of the world. We quickly arranged lodging at a hostel and walked down the tracks a mile or so to the Machu Picchu trailhead.

We discovered that there was a shuttle bus up to the ancient Incan city, but it cost several dollars. That was expensive for us. The ruins were situated far above the train tracks. We could see stone walls from where we were but had to look almost straight up to do so. It was a long way up there. The more I looked, the more it seemed like a good idea to take the shuttle!

Then Bob appeared at my elbow and said, "I like to walk a lot, and I want to walk up." I couldn't let him go alone, and he needed someone to translate for him if anything should happen, so he and I found the beginning of the trail and headed up. It was grueling. The trail didn't follow gentle contours to ease the climb. There were large boulders, and often the next step was waist high. Bob didn't seem to be having much trouble, but I was huffing and puffing. He kept an eye on me, and whenever I looked especially bad, he would claim to need a rest and would sit in some shade.

As we rested, Bob began to muse about the local people. He had read about them in preparation for the trip, and they were weighing heavily on his mind and spirit. He shared with me about their history and especially the great sacrifices they had made to serve the gods of those mountains. He compared this to modern Christians, not judgmentally, but with some sadness of spirit for our present lack of sacrificial commitment. We prayed for the Quechuas, descendants of the Incas.

As we went up the mountain, we stopped to rest several times, and Pastor Bob's reflections kept going deeper. I began to feel the authenticity and power of his faith. I sensed the brooding presence of God as he prayed. Wisdom and authority permeated his words as he talked. It was like I was on the mountain with Moses.

We had an amazing day. A local college student guided us through the ruins. The stonework was stunning. The layout of the place was intelligent and beautiful. The setting in the mountains was spectacular. The story of that specific city was fascinating. Our guide had recently turned from Catholicism to serve the ancient Incan gods of the mountains, and we had a warm and illuminating conversation with him about the revelations from God to the last king of the Incas before the Spaniards arrived. (You can read about those revelations in Don Richardson's book *Eternity in Their Hearts*.) We walked miles up and down the ancient streets and finally returned to Aguas Calientes, satisfied and weary.

There are natural hot springs there, and we went to soak a little. Bob came along. However, when we decided to get a pizza, he didn't go with us. He returned to the hostel for what we thought would be a well-deserved rest.

The next morning we gathered at the edge of the train tracks and had coffee and rolls while we waited for the train back to Cuzco. Bob wasn't there, but soon Alcir, his roommate and a member of our group, came walking up. He was shaking his head as he sat down at our table.

He explained that he had been concerned about Bob's age and health, so all through the night he would awaken about every hour to see if the pastor was all right. Every time he looked, Bob was not sleeping. He was on his knees praying for the people of those mountains. As far as Alcir could tell, Bob hadn't slept all night. At about that moment in our conversation, Bob came walking up looking calm and well.

We finished our breakfast just as the train pulled in. We got on and headed for Cuzco.

After we settled into our seats, Bob found someone who spoke English and started to share Jesus with him. The conversation seemed to be an enjoyable one. I stopped looking and started a conversation about life and meaning with a Peruvian named Jesus.

When both of us were quiet, I turned to Bob. I told him that if I tried to stay up all night and pray, not only would I spend most of my time trying not to give in to sleep, but also my efficiency would be near zero the next day. Eventually, I might even get sick.

He told me not to copy his actions but to follow the grace.

I didn't really understand but saw at least a glimmer of what he was saying. We can't produce faith, but we can respond to God's giving. We can cultivate His presence. We can nurture an inner atmosphere that grows faith. We can take steps of obedience that bring us to new levels in our faith. We can refuse to be satisfied with the faith that we have and seek God. We can submit ourselves to the means of grace and so be receptive to God. We can search for the pleasures that are found at His right hand (Ps. 16:11). In that joy we will be drawn with His cords of love (John 6:44; Heb. 11:4). Each of us can seek the particular mix that God has tailored to us. As we find satisfaction, we will seek more.

I never saw Bob again, but some months later I was telling the story of our trip to a wonderful woman of God, Joy Dawson. She began to laugh and said that Bob was a friend of hers. She told me the story of his church. This was something that Bob hadn't mentioned to me.

It seems that Bob had a normal church but that he wasn't satisfied with normal. He wanted more and persisted in asking God how it could be better. What could be done? Was there anything that God would ask of him? Finally he felt that God was telling him that he needed to pray more. In obedience to God's leading he began to sleep one night and pray through the next, alternating a night of prayer and a night of sleep through weeks and then months. After about six months the manifest presence of God came and filled Bob's church. The church filled with young people who were coming to faith. It was a vital and supernatural place.

Bob didn't tell me to pray one night and sleep the other. He told me to follow the grace. God has a different race marked out for each of us, and each of us can find the flow that brings us the deepest joy and pleasure. Faith is supposed to grow for us all. God's grace gives not only the leading but also the enablement as we obey.

It's all a gift (Eph. 2:8), but it goes dormant if not pursued. Many times in my life I've given remarkably little attention to the care and feeding of my faith. This even though I knew well the biblical truth that "the just shall live by faith" (Rom. 1:17; Gal. 3:11; Heb. 10:38). Everything depends on keeping the flame alive. It's Christ in us that is our hope of glory (Col. 1:27). How could anything be more important or more valuable?

When I was in my early teens, I read *To Build a Fire*, a novel by Jack London. In this story a relative newcomer to the far north of Alaska attempts a hike through the woods and up Henderson Creek to a camp where he would meet his friends. He is a man of no imagination and has an unexamined confidence in his ability to make the trip. He knew it would be cold but ignored the danger, not fully realizing it was 75 degrees below zero, or 107 degrees below freezing. The dog with him is a reluctant companion; canine instincts indicate it's too cold to travel.

As long as the man stays dry, he will be fine. Along the creek, though, there are springs that never freeze, and they leave thinly layered ice and unfrozen water under the snow. He manages to avoid them until lunch, when he builds a fire, eats, and warms up.

An old-timer had warned him that no one should travel alone with temperatures colder than fifty below zero. As he finished his lunch and lit his pipe, he felt confident. He thought, "Any man who is a man can travel alone."

About a half hour after he had resumed his journey, it happened. He broke through a thin crust of ice hidden under the snow and wetted his legs halfway to the knees. It was dangerous, but a fire would warm and dry him. He carefully constructed his tinder out of birch bark that he had in his pocket and dry driftwood that had collected at the edge of the creek bed. His fire got going, but he had made a mistake. He had built it under a spruce tree that was loaded with snow. His movements had disturbed the tree just enough that the snow on one bough tumbled down. It struck other branches and the process soon involved the whole tree. The fire was snuffed out in the cascading snow. Now the man's hands were numb with cold. He could no longer light a match to get the fire going.

In the rest of the story, Jack London details this man's growing panic and inability to overcome the freezing of his limbs and get another blaze going. It was too late. He tries to kill the dog to slice it open and warm his hands inside it, but he can't grasp his knife. He panics and runs, but has little stamina and falls repeatedly. Finally, he just settles down and embarks on what seems to him to be the deepest and most satisfying sleep of his life.

How many of us have suffered from the same lack of imagination and an overweening self-confidence in our spiritual lives? I have too often let the flame of my faith flicker and nearly go out just from a lack of care. God is gracious, and He wouldn't let us lose our faith because of an accident, like the man in this story lost his life. However, habitual neglect can have just as deadly an outcome. Many never wake up again. There are real dangers in the way of our spiritual journey, and we should never try to travel alone.

The trouble with self-help strategies that are so popular is that we simply don't have the resources in ourselves to achieve any kind of meaningful transformation, or even progress. They lure us with their promise of change—change that we can be proud of; change that we can have without immersing ourselves in Christ and giving up control of our lives; change that we can engage in with a satisfying sense of our own competence and goodness. But they don't work. The power and virtue must come from the person of Jesus. It can't come from anywhere else.

Jesus said that we must abide in Him (John 15:4–8). He goes so far as to say that without Him we can do nothing. Faith is not the force of our mind or the strength of will that we use to hold to our dogmas. It's Christ in us, the hope of glory. Our job isn't to try directly to have more faith. Our job is to abide in Christ and to obey His voice.

I have no satisfying explanation as to why more of us don't do that. Jesus is stimulating and creative beyond our ability to describe. As we look to Jesus, there is always more to discover, and pursuing

Him never gets old. He is intelligent beyond our comprehension. He is loving and kind. He can show us things that the eye has never seen and the ear has never heard. He invites us to work with Him in loving service that gives deep meaning to our lives. His presence is a place of aching beauty and sublime transcendence. How can we decline to pursue Him?

I suspect that one explanation of the mystery as to why so many of us don't diligently pursue God lies in the area of spirituality. I'm not talking about high morals but about how real the invisible is to us. It seems that, for most of us, heaven and the living, speaking, dynamic person of Jesus are mostly noble theories. In contrast, the world around us is very real. We get wrapped up in the immediate and doubt whether the profoundly spiritual is even relevant to the moment we're living in. With this doubt our pursuit is greatly weakened.

We need not neglect contemplating God and sitting in His presence. If we will answer God's invitation to seek Him, we will proceed from glory to glory (2 Cor. 3:18). This is not an impossible thing to do. He even promises to give us the desire to seek Him as He draws us to Himself (Phil. 2:13). All we have to do is pursue and not neglect this one necessary thing (Luke 10:41–42).

The potential of this life of faith is beyond our present comprehension, but even in what we can see there is satisfaction and wonder. In Jesus, Pastor Bob found transformative power that not only met his personal needs but also extended to his congregation and city. That same power is ours if only we will cultivate His presence.

6

Faith

Early in my YWAM training, before I met Pam or thought of Brazil, our School of Discipleship traveled to Redwood City, near San Francisco. There we were mixing our classroom time with action. For two or three weeks we were not only studying in a local church but also promoting an evangelistic concert, going to high schools and inviting students to come.

One afternoon we heard a lecture from a visiting speaker. He was a high school science teacher who had researched creationism and wanted to try it out on us. His goal was to teach it as an alternative to evolution in his classes. We were to be his friendly audience.

Almost as soon as he started talking, I realized that I knew more about the subject than he did. I had just finished my four-year course at Bethany Bible College and had taken a geology class my last semester. To complete that class I had written an eighty-page paper on the same subject. I had read or consulted a lot of books and material, probably more than an overworked teacher would have time to do.

During the whole afternoon, I constantly raised my hand and asked questions. I did this on the hardest bits, and he usually didn't know how to answer me. I had a pretty good idea that he wouldn't, since I hadn't come across anyone who had answers to my questions. I'm sure it must have been difficult for the teacher, but I wasn't noticing.

When the class was over and the speaker had left, we had more than an hour before dinner. I found a small, unused, windowless room in the church complex. In the room were several old pews with a hidden corner beyond them. It had become my practice to go there and pray in solitude.

On this evening I had just started to pray when God challenged me. I didn't hear a voice, and it was more of a communion of our spirits than words, but here is my attempt to recreate our interaction.

"What was that this afternoon?" He asked me.

"What do you mean, Lord?" I said. "It was a class."

"Yes, but what were you doing?"

"I asked a lot of questions."

I knew from the beginning of this exchange that I was in trouble, but it really hit me when God asked me why I had asked those questions. I hadn't analyzed anything during the class, but now it became painfully clear to me that I hadn't been looking for answers. I had been showing off. I struggled a little but soon admitted this to God. He was in the middle of challenging me to confess my sin of pride to the whole group when someone came down the hallway calling my name.

I had a telephone call and ran to answer it.

It was Danny Moody, the same friend who had taken me to the camp meeting so many years before. He wanted to see me, and we agreed that he would come to the coffeehouse where we would be meeting that night. The last time I'd seen Dan was when I was in the worst stage of my pitiful attempt to run from God. He hadn't been close to Jesus at that time either, and I certainly hadn't been any help to him. Now I wanted to let him know how well my walk of faith was going, and I was looking forward to seeing him. I went back to pray.

I started to pray for Dan, but God called me back to the issue of my pride and my need to confess it to the whole group. I argued that I shouldn't do it in front of my friend because I wanted him to be encouraged in his faith by my good testimony. Wouldn't that be damaged if I brought something so negative to light?

I didn't win the argument, though, and I finally told God that if I had a chance, I would confess that night. I told no one but God. I thought that might increase my chances of not having to say anything while Dan was there.

The evening came, and it was great to see my old friend. I tried hard to encourage Dan by talking about what God was doing for me. Then the more formal part of the evening started, and we had a worship service. It was just average and really a bit boring, but at least it didn't last forever.

The meeting was coming to an end, and I started to feel relieved that I hadn't needed to confess my pride in front of Dan and the group. But then, as our leader was getting ready to pray the closing prayer, he stopped. His eyes were closed, and he reached up and pinched the bridge of his nose, frowning with concentration.

"I believe that there's someone here tonight that needs to confess something to the group," he said. Then he put a chair in front of us all and continued, "Can that person come and sit here and confess?"

I was stunned, but I knew that it was me. I went right up and sat in the chair. I confessed my pride of that afternoon and asked for forgiveness.

We had some very traditional, earnest Christians in our group. They had been after me for a couple of months because I had long hair. Just days before my confession, one of them had claimed to know my motive for having long hair. According to him I wanted to impress certain kinds of women. I didn't think that was true, but it sure was irritating.

When I confessed my pride, those more traditional guys were among the first to come to pray for me. I couldn't help but notice the smug satisfaction on their faces. You could almost see them thinking that finally Jim was coming around! However, others who had become close friends also came, and everyone prayed with understanding and wisdom for me.

A move of God started and lasted two days. There was much confession of sin and prayer. Dan told me that before he left, he had finally seen the power that he read about in the New Testament. He was encouraged and strengthened to follow Jesus. God had gotten it right. He always does.

It's often hard for us to obey, though. We can't see the end from the beginning, and many times what God asks us to do goes against our self-interest. We're all faced regularly with the challenge of pursuing a life of faith or settling into something that isn't so demanding as walking with the living God.

Many settle. Some leave the Christian life altogether. Those that stay in church but slip away from a living faith tend to follow a certain religious way of life. There are millions of variations on the theme, but it usually goes something like the following.

Those who are born again start out with a supernatural, relational faith. God does everything for us, as a mother would for her baby. He expects little from us and just keeps pouring on the joy.

Then it gets harder. Is it just because the newness is wearing off, or is something else going on?

God wants us to learn to walk, so He takes a few steps away from us, holds out His arms to us, and waits. His intention is that we take our first steps in consciously exercising our faith. It's a time of momentous decision.

By now we're becoming aware that God can be demanding at times. We can't get Him under control. He asks us to do things that we don't want to do and to give up things that we want to hold on to. He insists that He is Lord and we're not. We clearly see that we can't have Him and at the same time keep control of our lives. There must be total surrender. It's only in that total surrender that we can ever live a life of faith and grow to our potential.

At this point many of us don't keep pressing. We start talking about how we don't live by feelings and settle into something that looks at first glance like a reasonable sort of middle way.

Pursuing intimacy with God can be a painful process. We can see the anguish of Isaiah in chapter 6 when he is placed before God on His throne. He has an almost unbearable revelation of his own uncleanness. This revelation demands repentance. Walking with God brings regular revelation about Him and about ourselves. Every time we get new light, we have to repent of how we thought or how we acted before. This can feel like we're losing too much that is comfortable and familiar as we step into an unknown future. We can experience frustration and fear as we work to give up so many ways of thinking and acting that have given us identity and security. We are not in control, and it's scary to trust someone else, even God.

In the Song of Solomon the young Shulamite woman calls out to the prince and he takes her to the palace. There they are married. They have their first night together in their chamber, and the bride sleeps. The prince leaves instructions that she isn't to be disturbed. When she awakens, he isn't beside her anymore. She hears his voice, but he is outside, leaping on the mountains. She likes the familiar place where they had their first night and speaks of him being outside "our wall." He, however, calls to her, "Rise up, my love, my fair one, / And come away" (Song of Sol. 2:10)

God is calling to us to rise up. We aren't to settle for past experiences and familiar surroundings in our walk of faith. He is outside, but it's not His intention to have a separation between us. He wants us to come outside and leap over the mountains with Him.

It's hard for us to give up the comforts of what we know so well and the warm memories of our first love.

God is relentless, though, and will settle for nothing less than the highest in our lives. Paul describes the process like this: "casting down arguments and every high thing that exalts itself against the knowledge of God, bringing every thought into captivity to the obedience of Christ" (2 Cor. 10:5). Many of us won't persevere in this demanding, unrelenting inner transformation, so we decide to substitute the actual presence of God with something else.

Some never consider these things, nor do they have a moment when they make a decision to back away. It often seems more like we have gradually lost touch with God. We can't get a sense of Him. The light just doesn't seem to break through. We can't get close to God, but neither do we want to abandon His ways entirely.

Instead of pursuing intimacy with God, we manufacture something that we can control. Indeed, the issue of control often seems to be the defining battleground. It's much more familiar and feels more manageable to do it on our own. After all, aren't we able to stand (1 Cor. 10:12)? Those of us that won't give up control of our lives must live out something that is not faith. That is, it is not relational and revelatory in its essence.

In this aloneness, we must create something that will give a context to our service for God. We systematize and dogmatize our best understanding of good and evil and create codes of conduct, religious ritual, measures of dedication, and comparative standards of behavior. Our theology often comes to focus more on legal questions of escaping punishment for our sins than on pursuing a loving, transformational relationship with God.

We gradually build all this dogma, doctrine, codes of conduct, religious culture, and ritual into what can be an impressive-looking structure of beliefs. We dedicate the whole thing to God and adopt it as our way of serving the Lord. This will mean that we look like acceptable Christians, so it's nice socially. However, there's little or no enlightening, intimate dialogue with God. This is no longer faith, with love at the center. We might look okay on the surface, but there is not much life going on.

Most of the pain, inconvenience, and struggle of walking continually with the living God is gone, but so is most of the life, the joy, the peace, and the sublime beauty.

This seems to be so pervasive among Christians that it will usually be seen as normal. It often appears that even pastors and Christian leaders assimilate little at Bible college and seminary except the ability to build a more professional-looking version of religious structure for their lives.

This is what happened to me. I came out of Bible college after four years with almost no living relationship with God. This was not the school's fault. It was how I reacted to the learning offered there and to other distractions. I wasn't living by the sublime, dynamic, relational faith that God had given me years before in that camp meeting. I deserved to be abandoned by the Lord, but He didn't leave me.

A couple of months after I graduated, God broke through immediately after a conversation with my chess-playing neighbor. I couldn't deny Him. I prayed and received a dim, uncertain impression that I should go to Youth With A Mission. Once again God made Himself known to me. He instructed me, and I knew enough to obey. His graciousness is so piercing, sublime, and revolutionary. It's unrelenting, undeserved, and indescribable.

When I got to YWAM, everything was centered on the person of God. We were taught to meditate on the Bible, focusing on hearing God in the Word and knowing Him better. We learned to pray by listening a lot more and talking only after we had heard from Him. Our classes were about His character and ways. It was the person and character of God from morning to evening, not only in theory but also in practice.

This was threatening to the internal religious structures that I had worked hard to build up in myself over the years. I had dedicated them to God. In my mind they represented my devotion to Him. The focus on God speaking to us produced a flutter of excitement in me, but it seemed unreliable. I had seen examples of people who said that God had spoken to them when it seemed obvious that they were using His name to do what they wanted. I didn't reject the possibilities that were being presented to me in class, but I suspended judgment and didn't decide right away if this was the way to live.

There was a guy in YWAM that I only saw occasionally. He worked in a different location from where we were studying, and I never knew when he might show up. His name was Ivan, and he was a joyful, sincere pursuer of Jesus. Just about every time he saw me, Ivan would ask, "Jim, what is Jesus saying to you?"

This was awkward, because Jesus wasn't saying anything to me. I knew how to do Bible studies and term papers. I knew how to make sermon outlines. I could rip propositional truth out of the scriptural narrative and organize it into a system of belief. I had a well-developed cognitive approach to truth but very little ongoing experience or dialogue with God. I didn't know how to receive living instruction from God through the Bible. I was approaching it with an Enlightenment epistemology, attitude, and set of tools. There was little of the dimension of faith. And I was pretty much blind to all of this. To me, my approach seemed dependable, while Ivan's approach seemed unreliable.

One morning I was thinking that Ivan was about due to come around. I didn't want to be embarrassed yet again, so I decided that I would try meditating on the Bible as we had been taught. I asked God to speak to me from Scripture.

He did! It wasn't mental gymnastics or the clever application of Greek logic and philosophy. The Word was opened to me in a way that fit me perfectly. The Holy Spirit was guiding me into all truth. He was edifying me. My time in the Word wasn't professional and academic. It was an exercise of living faith. The Bible became exciting to me because it was a place to meet with God and dialogue with Him.

Ivan did come over that day, and we had a tremendous conversation. Jesus had actually said something to me, and I was excited about it.

I started to break through in other areas as well. I was rediscovering authentic spirituality as opposed to mere religious performance. I was closer to God, and I was starting to live by faith again. I began to be less of a hypocrite and was learning to be strengthened by God (Eph. 3:14–21) and to live what I believed. This growth is still going on, and it's centered on faith—the living, ongoing, dynamic experiencing of God Himself, with a response of trust and obedience coming from me.

Pam and I are close friends with a YWAM couple God called into the depths of the Amazon jungle to reach out to the Banawá people. As soon as their basic training was finished, Daniel and Fátima set out. To get there, they had to travel for weeks on various riverboats, with long waits in between boat rides. Finally, the day came when they arrived in the settlement closest to the tribe.

It was a tiny village made up of people who lived off the jungle: hunting and fishing, tilling small plots of manioc, and doing a little commerce with the trading boats that occasionally got that far into the wilderness. No one wanted to risk their life taking Daniel and Fátima to the Indian village. This tribe had a fearsome reputation.

Finally, the leader of the river village said he would do it. They set out in two small canoes down the Piranhas River to where a smaller stream fed into the larger waterway. They headed up that small stream into the depths of the dark jungle. A short time later their guide told them that the village was now easy to find. They just had to continue upstream.

He would go no further and headed back toward his settlement. They continued on alone. Daniel told me that he was pretty sure they would die that day, but that they believed that Jesus was worth any sacrifice and that they had to obey the Lord.

They found the village and they didn't die, though things between them and the Banawá were extremely tense for a while. After some months they began to be accepted, and the tribe taught them how to live in the jungle. Daniel and Fátima began to help the tribe in return.

Half of the Banawá babies were dying each year, so Fátima trekked out of the jungle and got training as a midwife. She studied nutrition and convinced the mayor of the nearest town, a five-day boat ride away, to give them vitamins. No more babies died.

The Banawá ate mostly proteins like fish and game and had little agriculture. Daniel, an agricultural technician, searched out edible plants that would grow in the Amazon and began to plant them for Fátima, who for medical reasons needed to have a lot of fiber in her diet. The Banawá began to trade meat and fish with Daniel for seedlings that they could plant, and the seasonal hunger of the tribe became a thing of the past. The tribe, which had been on the edge of extinction, was now holding its own. Most of the young men were alcoholics, though, and no marriages were happening.

One day, years after their arrival, Daniel and Fátima were jogging through the jungle on a pig hunt. Daniel was in the front, cutting his way through thick growth with a machete. Suddenly a poisonous snake sprang out of the undergrowth and sunk its fangs into Fátima's leg. She screamed and Daniel ran to her. He shot the snake and then turned to Fátima, tearing her pant leg away from the bite. The fang marks were clear. Daniel sliced across them with his machete and began to suck out blood and poison, his heart sinking because he knew that this would not be enough to save her. When he had done all that he could, Daniel put Fátima on his shoulders, and dragging the snake with them, he headed back to the village.

When the Indians saw the snake and heard what had happened, they reacted with great sorrow and began to mourn for
Fátima. They were sure that she would die.

Daniel took her into their house and laid her on the bed, his
heart beating hard with fear and sorrow. She asked him for water,
so he grabbed a container and headed for the stream.

As soon as she was alone, Fátima began to entreat the Lord,
"Father, I can't die yet. The Banawá have been blessed in many
ways, but they don't know you. If their lives don't change, they will
cease to exist as a tribe. Our work isn't finished."

The Lord said, "I've been wanting to talk to you about that.
When you were starting out, your priority was your relationship
with me. Now your first thought is about finishing a task. You're
full of duty and obligations but no longer so close to me as you
used to be. Fátima, I want your heart back."

Fátima felt herself enveloped in God, and her immediate reaction was to confess and repent. "Oh Lord," she said, "please forgive
me for forgetting that our relationship is why You created me. I
want you more than anything, and I repent of my lack of seeking. I
now turn my attention totally to seeking and loving you."

As soon as she finished praying, her leg began to burn. It
burned until she could barely stand it. By the time Daniel got back
with water, she had been healed. The next day she walked down to
the stream and got her own water.

Fátima chose the sublime. She got back the beauty and wonder.
She returned to a focus on "Christ in you, the hope of glory" (Col.
1:27). When I talk to her today, I get the distinct impression that
her renewed relationship with Christ has stuck in her mind far
more than the healing.

There's no life in codes of conduct. There's no joy in measur-
ing our dedication and that of others by how well we measure up
to particular understandings of biblical standards. When we try to
live that way, it's a life of religion, but you would be hard-pressed to

find any significant relational, faith dynamic. We can't get enough spiritual nutrition out of a religion that isn't centered on intimacy with God (Gal. 3:21).

Life flows from Jesus. We must know Him as the bread of life (John 6:50–51). We must live by feeding on Him (John 6:53–57).

When we lack that flow but have a religious life that we dedicate to God, it doesn't produce a good outcome. We will lack buoyancy and joy. This produces insecurity and dissatisfaction. Instead of abundant life, we have religious obligation and an inner hunger. In our attempts to fill that hunger, we find that comparing ourselves favorably to others brings some relief.

So we will judge those around us in an attempt to squeeze some kind of life out of our religion. Even when we try to love others, we fail because we're in deep need ourselves, and our focus settles on getting rather than giving love. There are millions of personal variations on this theme, but they are all a miserable way to live.

The power of Jesus's resurrected life in us is what gives life and produces righteousness. Paul said that if Christ didn't rise from the dead, then our faith is empty and we (Christians) are of all people the most miserable (1 Cor. 15:12–19). In Galatians 3:21 Paul writes, "If there had been a law given which could have given life, truly righteousness would have been by the law."

Anything we do to forge an easier, less demanding spiritual life is doomed to fail. We can't get enough life out of it, so we start to create circumstances through which we feel like we might be receiving life. Superiority feels good, so we begin to compare ourselves with others. This generates insecurity, so we begin to compete. We all want to win, so we don't play fair anymore.

Pretty soon we have an accusatory religious mess full of judgmental attitudes and hypocritical attempts to impress. This brings anxiety and stress. It is common in this situation to make sacrifices for God and His cause, but we get little or no life or joy from this effort. The good we want to do we don't do. The bad that we want to avoid seems to always prevail (Rom. 7:18–23). Relief can only come through the living Spirit working in us (Rom. 8:1–5).

Sometimes this sort of life is precipitated by an attempt to create distance from the pain and inconvenience of God's push to transform us. When Moses called the people to meet with God on the mountain, they didn't want to. They asked Moses to go alone, speak to the Lord, and then tell them what God had said. They found God too overwhelming and didn't want to deal with God or have Him interfere with their desires. They retreated into a position that guaranteed distance. Many of us do this today.

Some of us never have a moment when we consciously make this decision. It's more like we lose touch with God. We can't get a sense of Him. The light just doesn't seem to break through. Isaiah 50:10–11 talks about those who walk in darkness, without a light, and exhorts them to trust in God. It goes on to recognize that some won't do this. They would rather light their own fire and walk by its light. God's conclusion regarding these people is that they will "lie down in torment."

Fátima was busy serving God and partially lost the walk of faith and intimacy for a time. It would be hard to find anyone more dedicated to God's cause, but she had drifted from the life of dynamic intimacy. She came back, much as many of us have done. God also moved in the people in the tribe, and today 80 percent of them are living a life of faith in Jesus. Alcoholism is no longer devastating the young men. People are getting married, and babies are being born. This is the result of faith.

Paul concludes in Romans 14:23, "Whatsoever is not from faith is sin." Authentic Christian spirituality demands, even consists of, living by faith. Faith is the relational dynamic that gives us access to personal experience with God. This is a constant pursuit that must never stop.

God is infinite. No matter how much I might know of Him, there is infinitely more to learn. He is perfect beauty, energy, power, order, understanding, love, glory, wisdom, humility, meekness, knowledge, wonder, faithfulness, compassion, and even suffering. Why do we rebel against such a perfect God? The "mystery of law-lessness" (2 Thess. 2:7) is complex and chaotic by origin and by nature; it's mysterious in why it happened and how it has developed. Certainly one of the most opaque, indecipherable, and unyielding aspects of this mystery is that so many of us don't choose to pursue God.

We so often would rather hold on to our little, controllable expressions of religiosity. We fear losing control. We hold to sources of security that are based in strategies we have developed to pro-tect ourselves in a dangerous world. We rebel against giving up our willfulness. We love certain kinds of darkness and don't want God to shed light on them.

The life of faith is one of abandonment. This is an adventure of letting God take us to places that we've never seen and that we can't even imagine. Indescribable beauty and joy await those who dare to trust God and run this race that is set before us (Heb. 12:1–2). It's only in this pursuit of faith, this clinging to the person of God and doing everything with Him, that we will find transformation and life (Gal. 3:21).

7

Authenticity

I was in Hawaii in late 1974 and had just gotten engaged to Pam. My friend Ivan was on the island of Oahu for a few months. This was the same friend that had the habit of asking me what Jesus was saying to me. He got in touch with me, and we decided to go to Makapu'u beach that Saturday to do a little bodysurfing. I could meet his new wife, and he could meet my fiancée.

Saturday dawned windy, and the surf was big. We were soon on the beach talking and having a good time getting to know the new members of our little group of four. With the surf so high, there were red warning flags everywhere, flapping in the wind.

I didn't want to swim, but I also didn't want to be the one to chicken out. I thought I could avoid both, so I asked Ivan, "Are we going to bodysurf?"

I figured that if Ivan had any sense at all, he would point out that the surf was dangerous that day and that we should not go in. Then he would be the one seen as being afraid, and I would be able to graciously agree. However, I guess he was concerned with the same issues, so he said, "I don't know, are we?"

I mumbled something like, "That's why we came, isn't it?"

We walked into the surf like lambs to the slaughter. Neither of us wanted to, but neither did we want to admit that we didn't want to. We had to live up to a masculine code of courage. Maybe we were afraid that the girls would think less of us.

At least we had the good sense to go where a group of locals were bodysurfing. We figured that they would know the currents. Soon we were struggling with all our might just to survive.

The waves were huge, and we had to dive under them in just the right way. They were so big that it took a long time to get through one and come up for air. No sooner would we gasp in some oxygen than the next wave would come. It was not fun, and I didn't see anyone who got enough time in between waves to catch the next one. To complicate things, there were waves reflecting in from an adjacent cliff, so we were getting it from two sides.

At one point I looked up between waves, and it seemed that the beach was getting an awfully long ways away. I decided to swim in to shore and get out of the surf. Putting my head down, I swam as strongly as I could, being careful to keep one eye on the waves behind me. Just as I was getting into full effort, a hand pushed on the top of my head, stopping me. I looked up, indignant, and saw a fit-looking guy.

"What do you think you are doing?" I demanded to know.

"I'm a life guard, and I need to talk to all of you," he said.

He got our group of ten or so together and explained to us that we were in a six-mile-an-hour current that was taking us out to sea. We needed to swim to the side to get around the current and make our way to shore. As I was floating and listening, my foot came out of the water. He saw that I didn't have fins.

"What are you doing out here today without fins?" he asked sharply. We didn't answer. "Just take a forty-five-degree angle toward shore and swim until you make progress," he said and began to swim away.

"Wait a minute," I said. "Do you think we can make it without fins?"

"I don't know," he said, "but I can't help you in this surf."

We swam for an hour and a half before we finally felt the sand under our feet. All I could think of the whole time was that I was not going to die before I married Pam!

Ivan and I had felt the need to impress, so we were both dishonest about our reluctance to go into the water.

I suppose that most of us have struggled with a tendency to want to impress others, to create a false impression that inflates our worthiness or value in some way. Sometimes it's innocent, like at the beach, but it can become a web of falsehood that leaves us unable to trust one another in our relationships. Even though all of us have failed when seduced by this temptation, we also instinctively hate falsehood, especially the kind that expresses itself as religious hypocrisy.

We end up not thinking much of ourselves. The lower the opinion we have of ourselves, the more we feel a need to be loved and esteemed by others. This creates a powerful draw for even more approval, which leads to more hypocrisy. It's the frustration and failure that Paul describes in Romans 7 as he talks about his religious life as a Pharisee, when he was trying to perfect himself through rules and regulations and not by faith.

In this striving to impress, there is a built-in need to tear other people down. *Maybe I'm not perfect, but I'm better than a lot of people. If I can just bring down everyone around me, maybe people will notice that I'm doing pretty well.* We become judgmental and love to gossip, especially in a religious setting that puts a lot of value on performing and keeping the rules. We operate just like the Pharisees.

Have you ever been in a conversation where you are saying harsh things about someone in the form of a prayer request and that person walks into the room? The terrible silence that ensues is the awkwardness of being caught in betrayal. You act like a friend when you're with that person, but if they're not there, you try to show that they are not as good as you. This is pitiful but common among us.

We (humanity in general) are also prone to fill up our essential emptiness inside by resorting to false comforts. Drugs, sex, esteem from others, material goods, and belonging to a particular group come to mind, but there are many others as well. We try to resist, but the need is always there. It wears us down, and we finally do whatever it is that we've been longing to do.

You won't win in the long term if you are empty.

Of course, we want to hide what we have done from other Christians, so we start a life in the shadows. It's a life of sins, and we don't mention it. But we know that we're not authentic and our faith is crippled. We feel profoundly uneasy around God, so we don't seek Him like we used to. We fear that others will discover our falseness, so we get a bumper sticker that says, "Not perfect, just forgiven."

When I was five or six years old, my friends and I wanted to be scientists. We didn't have a lab or chemistry set, but one day we found a way to pursue our fascination with experimentation. The groundskeeper had swept up pine needles, branches, and pinecones in a pile and burned them. It had pretty much burned out, but there were some live coals. Fire is dynamic. We thought it would be great for some experiments. We also knew that adults wouldn't approve of us playing with fire, so we hid in a storage shed to do our thing.

Soon we had three fires going, one for each of us. We built them on the wooden shelves in the shed but were confident we could control them with damp sawdust that was just outside the door. We happily burned various things and wrote down the color and smell of the smoke. We felt ourselves on the frontiers of scientific discovery!

At one point I looked behind me. My friend had let his fire get too big. I lunged out the door and plunged my hands into the sawdust. Excited and in a hurry, I got my hands too deep in the pile and was soon throwing very fine, dry sawdust on the fire—not a good way to put it out.

This wasn't working, so I ran across the street to our house where I quickly filled a small glass and a teacup with water. I spilled most of it on my way back, and when I did get to the shed, my friends were gone. Inside, a wall was now on fire. I threw my few drops of water on it and ran.

We had caused a disaster, and I was concerned about getting caught. What could I do to put myself in the best possible light? My mom was always trying to get me to take naps, and I was always resisting. I thought that it would look good if I voluntarily lay down in the afternoon. I went up to my room and got onto my bed. They would find me here and my innocence would be indisputable.

As I lay there, I could hear the growing commotion outside. Burney, our town, was so small that we had a volunteer fire department. There was one main street in town, and when there was a fire, men raced up and down it calling everyone to come help put it out. I heard the siren and the excited conversation going on outside. It finally occurred to me that it was unnatural for me to be in my bed at such a time. It would look suspicious, so I got up and went outside.

This looked like one of the biggest social events of the year. Everyone was there. Even my aunt and uncle had seen the smoke and come into town from their ranch. People were milling around and watching the firemen work. Then I saw my dad. He was facing the fire and had his back to me. Normally I would have liked to see him, but not now. I had something to hide and didn't want him around.

I kind of squirmed up beside him and commented on the fire without making eye contact. My guilt must have been obvious, but I didn't know that. He turned to me and asked, "Jimmy, did you have anything to do with this?" Astounded by his insight, I confessed. I got into big trouble, of course, and it was a while before I was at ease around Dad.

So many of us are more or less avoiding God because our religious efforts have failed and we have things to hide. We need to get back to a place of transparent honesty with Him. Then the inner life that gives us the victory can be restored to its full flow.

How can that happen? It's the way of faith, being so full of God's presence that the reality of our well-being and fullness takes away the need to impress or to seek out false comforts. In the light of God's glory, greatness, and worthiness, no opinions other than His can discourage us. It's not worth it to impress people if the price is His disapproval. His life in us fills us with satisfaction and joy.

God's grace comes to us by faith and takes on whatever form we need to face our immediate challenges. This works best if we have some understanding of the multifaceted nature of His grace and its major expressions. What is the appropriate form of grace we need to attain authenticity in our Christian spirituality?

The heart of authenticity is the fear of God. This fear is not something that we can think up or generate in ourselves, and yet God demands it of us. In 2 Corinthians 7:1 we read, "Having these promises, beloved, let us cleanse ourselves from all filthiness of the flesh and spirit, perfecting holiness in the fear of God." It's what happened to Isaiah when he saw God on His throne, confessed his sin, was purified, and offered to go in obedience to the Lord (Isa. 6:1–9). It's what happened to Job when he went through so much adversity and then was confronted and questioned by God. At the end of the process Job said, "I have heard of You by the hearing of the ear, / But now my eye sees You. / Therefore I abhor myself, / And repent in dust and ashes" (Job 42:5–6).

Jesus is our best example of authenticity. He didn't care at all about being famous. He was at His most confrontational when the crowds were the greatest (John 6). He knew that He pleased the Father, and that was enough. This was the basis of His authenticity.

He didn't fear those that could only kill the body, but He did counsel us to fear Him who can destroy both body and soul in hell (Matt. 10:28).

What do you fear, respect, or reverence? Those who fear rejection and revere recognition will never be authentic. And we will always end up failing in our authenticity if we are empty. Only by being full of the Spirit is our satisfaction deep enough that we don't need to impress.

One of the keys to authenticity in our lives is to be concerned with the opinion of only one, Jesus. No one else can properly pass judgment on us, whether that judgment is negative or positive. If we are in some way dependent on the opinions and judgments of others, we will be strongly compelled to perform. In that performance there will be much that is false. You cannot successfully perform to impress God. He knows all.

Here is the heart of the fear of the Lord, to be utterly convinced that everything we do is in the revealing light of His presence and knowledge. The only way to be genuinely convinced of that, to the point that it's part of the fiber of our being, is through experiencing the presence of God. This is what happened to both Isaiah and Job.

We experience reverential awe and deep affection. The respect that is generated is so deep that it becomes a high priority to please Him. He won't let us get away with anything, because His goals for us are so high and His love for us is so deep. When we experience this, we have the beginnings of wisdom (Prov. 9:10). When we are convinced in every fiber of our being, we hate any form of evil (Prov. 8:13).

His grace has come to us in the form of the fear of God, and we put aside hypocrisy, lies, and attempts to impress. We become authentic.

Francisco, Part 3

You will remember that the rebel officer demanded Francisco kill for them as the cost of his life. As he then offered the AK-47 machine gun, Francisco, battered and bruised from all of the torture, looked him in the eye and said, "I am a servant of Jesus. The Bible, His Word, says, 'You shall not kill.' I understand what you want me to do, but I can't. I must obey God rather than you."

The commander was furious. He commanded his soldiers to return him to lock-up. The next day, they opened the cell and led him to the area behind the jail.

One of them said, "You dig right here, and keep digging until we tell you that you can stop."

Francisco started digging. He dug through that day and the next. Finally, the hole was so deep that his head was a couple of meters underground when he was standing in it. At that point, he was told he could stop digging.

They called the commander and he said to Francisco, "Throw the shovel up here." Francisco had to give it quite a heave to get it up and out of the hole.

The commander gave the shovel to the soldiers and told them to fill the hole, staying to watch. When the dirt was up to Francisco's shoulders, he stopped them and spoke to Francisco again.

"It's up to you. If you will take the gun and kill for us, we will still let you go. We will believe that you are not a government agent. If you won't kill for us, then we are going to finish filling up the hole. We are going to bury you alive."

Francisco, standing trapped in the hole with dirt covering his body up to his neck, said, "Do whatever you have to do. I must obey Jesus."

The commandant threw his hands up in the air and said, "I don't know why I don't kill you." He turned to the soldiers and told them to dig Francisco up. They did so and then threw him back in jail.

A few days later, word came that a column of the government army was coming. The rebel forces had decided they couldn't defend Ganda and began to leave. One of the last things they did as they left town was to free all prisoners.

Francisco was out of jail. The government army was coming to town. What, he wondered, would the future hold for him?

8

Unity

In John 17 we have Jesus's high priestly prayer. As He pours out His heart to the Father just hours away from the crucifixion, we see the Trinity. God is one, yet here Jesus the Son is praying in the Spirit to the Father, the others in the inseparable unity of the Godhead. This theme is strongest in verses 20–26.

The triune nature of God means that reality, even before creation, has always been inseparable from interpersonal dynamics. This relational dimension is at the very root of what is. The universe in which we live came from the relational matrix of the Trinity. There never was a proud, isolated, and splendidly independent being out of whom came all that is. All that is came out of family.

This isn't the place to engage in depth the concepts and reality of the Trinity, but the fact of the divine family working together in creation has profound implications for our lives today.

God is Father, Son, and Holy Spirit. He celebrates both diversity and unity. There is room for diversity. There is joy and power in unity. Only the reality of the Trinity produces this sublime combination.

Here we see that friendship, including family, is important. We were not made to be more and more independent. The kind of unfettered liberty that comes out of separation from others is a phantom that seems to promise freedom and happiness but can't deliver. This increasing investment in personal autonomy sometimes seems to be one of the major directions of Western culture, but it is misguided. You won't find what you need by becoming more and more distant from others.

We were made to belong. Ephesians 1:5–6 says that God "predestined us to adoption as sons by Jesus Christ to Himself, according to the good pleasure of his will, to the praise of the glory of His grace, by which He made us accepted in the Beloved." We were created for adoption. We were created to be part of the family.

In John 17:21–23 Jesus prays "that they all may be one, as You, Father, are in Me, and I in You; that they also may be one in Us, that the world may believe that You sent Me. And the glory which You gave Me I have given them that they may be one just as We are one."

When God created us, He wasn't motivated by anything that we were going to produce or anything that He would get out of us. He created us out of pure generosity, for inclusion in the life that He has had since eternity past. He has always experienced perfect joy, peace, and mutual enjoyment in the family of the Trinity—perfect unity of heart and purpose, satisfaction, and fulfillment. By nature He is generous, so He wanted to share the inexpressible, sublime wonder of His family. Out of that pure benevolence He created us.

One could say of a car that it was made for driving. In this sense it is proper to say, as many remind us, that God created us in such a way that it is good for us to worship Him and glorify His name. It is a function to which we are suited, and we must do it if we want to become what God created us to be. We find our place in the order of things when we clearly see who God is. Worship opens our eyes so that we can see Him. This is of highest importance and has priority over all other activities.

Worship is one of the primary ways to know God, to get close to Him so that His glory and grace will produce His nature in us (2 Pet. 1:2–4). For that reason we need to worship for our own good. God has no need of being reminded that He is good. There is no insecurity in Him that needs affirmation. He didn't create us so that we could supply something that was missing. But without worship, something is missing in us.

God created us to be part of His family. I'm not speaking of what we were created to do (worship, serve, etc.) but of the pure motive of God's heart for creating us, which had nothing to do with what He would get out of it. He created us so that He could give us the wonder of full inclusion into perfect, unending love. The unpacking of how this would happen came later as God began to teach human beings the details of how to live.

That means we can participate fully and voluntarily in belonging to a loving family. Our whole design is aimed at this oneness. True friendship reflects reality that comes from before the earliest stirrings of human history. In friendship we have the context for the supreme fulfillment of our potential as human beings. This goes so deep that one could say that God builds His kingdom on friendships.

The structure of the kingdom of God has little in common with the governments that run countries. These are generally characterized by rigid power structures that function through impersonal bureaucracy. The purpose is to keep control, to make everyone keep the laws. They motivate by reward and punishment. You benefit if you keep the rules. You suffer if you don't. Often it is, at best, a mystery as to just whose interests are being served by government infrastructure.

God's rule is different. It is carried out through a vast network of friendships. It is loving and relational. Everyone has access to the highest authority with no layers of middle management. It is defined by promises and built by generosity of spirit, starting with God who gives His Spirit freely to us, God who floods our lives with the grace to live. We develop this kingdom as we submit to one another in love (1 Pet. 5:5). The power works through different expressions of His grace. Under this rule we fulfill the precept of the law through love that is imparted by the Holy Spirit (Rom. 8:4; Gal. 6:14).

It's not that God uses friendships as a strategy to build His kingdom. These relationships are the very substance of His reign, the essence of the kingdom for those who are a part of it. Loving friendships, unified by His life in us, are the building blocks that are a foundational part of its reality. Because of His life that runs through all who believe, we are all linked in profound ways that go beyond mutual respect or social interaction. This is a fascinating mystery, begging to be explored.

Everything that is came from and expresses relationship. When we try to understand the gospel as something meant primarily to define our individual legal standing before God, it brings strange distortions into our understanding. The glory of God isn't primarily His power. It is primarily His goodness (Exod. 34:6–7). Goodness is defined by our interaction in relationships (Rom. 13:8–10).

Today I listened to a song. The words of the song express the relief of the singer that God's grace has brought him forgiveness for his sins. The song goes on to say that he sins but it doesn't matter because God's grace is bigger than his sin. This is a terrible conclusion. Sin is sin because it violates love. That is why God recognizes it as sin (Rom. 13:8–10). If we harm others by sinning, it will always matter to a loving God. He will disapprove. His grace can't encourage this violation of love without violating His very nature. If we will think relationally and live by the grace that a life of faith brings to us, we will have the love of God poured out in our hearts (Rom. 5:5). This love is divine in its origins and empowers us to be authentically loving. The grace of God brings answers not only for my guilt but also for my transformation. This transformation is relationally defined.

Therefore, grace is not just to resolve a legal issue between God and me. It is also the means God uses to change me into someone who does no harm to others but loves them in word and in deed.

In John 17 Jesus prayed that we would be one as He and the Father are one. That certainly will not happen if the resources we use in our attempt to be so are only human. Jesus put this request in the context of our inclusion in Him. He makes the observation that He has given us His glory so that we can be one. It is not an ideology that is going to unite us, either with God or with each other. To the extent that we all spend time receiving His glory, the sum total of all that He is, we will be becoming one. It's Him in us and us in Him. That is the answer.

We can move toward unity and friendship that is powerfully transcendent only because we are first in Him. We are only able to be in Him if we walk by faith. Faith is the gift of the capacity to see, hear, know, experience, and respond in obedience to God. It's in our knowing, experiencing, and responding to Him that everything else happens. Without friendship with God we can't aspire to the unity Jesus prayed for.

On the other hand, without a human touch of friendship, few would find Him. Indeed, John tells us that if we don't love our brother who we see, we cannot love God, who we don't see (1 John 4:20). We should not think that we can live out our faith in splendid isolation. We need to exercise faith in community, or the whole process is short-circuited. Our love for God and our love for one another are so intertwined that they can never be separated.

When I was a freshman in high school, I made a friend, the same friend I spoke of in earlier chapters of this book, Dan Moody. His family opened their hearts, their lives, and their home to me. Between my freshman and sophomore years, my mom was going to go to San Francisco to study for her master's degree. I didn't want to go and talked about it to Dan. He came up with a plan.

There was a cattle ranch on the northern California coast at a place called Bear Harbor. It was a wild and isolated place, rugged and beautiful. It was just what I wanted for the summer. The amazing thing is that his family invited me to stay with them so that we could take a job at that ranch. My mom agreed to let me go.

Dan and I worked together through that summer, building fences, doing repairs, painting the farmhouse, and trying to keep out of the way of fighting bulls. During our off hours we explored the beaches, streams, and ponds on the ranch. What a summer!

Dan's family was devout. We stayed at the ranch during the week but would go to town on the weekend and attend church on Sunday. The church services were generally boring to me, and I didn't understand them. Sitting there every Sunday morning wasn't much fun, but it was worth the price to get a summer like that one.

Dan and his family were full of love and warmth. They had lost their home in a flood the previous winter and were living in a trailer while they built a new house. I didn't know where they found the extra time and energy to include a boy like me in their family life.

The weeks went by, and I began to know the other people at church. Sheldon, the pastor's son, befriended me. He was a couple of years older and had a pure, loving spirit of devotion to God. I found him fascinating and knew that there was something different about him.

By the end of August, it was the most natural thing in the world for me to speak to God about the love that these people had toward one another and toward me. That's when Jesus came to me and gave me faith. I began my adventure of knowing Him.

Through the next several years as I began to establish myself in the Lord, those friends were there. On one level my story is one of divine intervention. On another it is a story of human friendship.

We can't develop our love for God without growing in our love for others. There is no living this life of faith while not loving people. First John 4:20–21 says, "If someone says, 'I love God,' and hates his brother, he is a liar; for he who does not love his brother whom he has seen, how can he love God whom he has not seen? And this commandment we have from Him: that he who loves God must love his brother also." Our experience of God is transformational, generating love for others within us. The love we receive from others is a source of God's love for us. One love feeds the other. They both come from the source, Jesus.

In His prayer Jesus asks the Father "that they also may be one in Us, that the world may believe that you sent Me." Dan and his family and Sheldon and his family were that to me. It snuck up on me, but it finally happened exactly as Jesus prayed.

All of this won't happen if we are just walking around pretending to love one another and trying to do correct things according to our definitions of love. We will only find our oneness with each other when we are in Him. We will only find it by faith. He takes us into Himself. He takes up residence in us. We are no longer trying hard to act as we should; rather, Christ is in us and shares His nature with us, empowering us to obey. God is love, and our lives will be filled with and express love to the extent that we are in Him.

This is at the heart of God's strategy to reach out to the world to include all peoples in His generosity. When we are full of this reality, a reality that comes only by Jesus in us, the Lord becomes visible to those who don't yet know Him. I saw something different in the people at Dan's little country church, and that became my point of contact with God. This has happened millions of times around the world throughout church history. The more powerful our unity, the more deeply we belong to one another, the more Jesus is revealed to the world.

The other things we do are nothing more than a framework. Our thorough planning, careful organizing, incisive decision making, and painstaking problem solving are just so many dead bones if there is no life. Our terrifying sacrifices and exhausting efforts will only produce big monuments to strife if it isn't all permeated with His Spirit. Unity only comes by immersion together in God. It only comes in a life of faith.

If you are on a spiritual journey that is leading you into greater isolation from others, stop and reevaluate. Maybe what you are experiencing has been twisted into something that doesn't come from God.

All of us want to have loyal friendships and be included in a circle of deep fellowship. People who know Jesus want to be a part of bringing justice and resources to a needy world. We want people to come to know Jesus. These things being so, we must learn to come out of the shadows, out of the illusion that Christian life consists of carefully keeping the rules (Col. 2:16–23). Keeping the rules doesn't produce love, or life, or unity. These are only experienced in the reality of the person of God. The wonder only happens when we live by faith.

This life of faith is not an isolated existence. As we walk by faith, other people will contribute to the life of Jesus in us. His life in us will become rivers of living water, flowing out to others. Sometimes we will experience Him in prayer, worship, or meditation on the Word. At other times we will get life from people who are in our lives. A life of faith is a life of enlightening, genuine, enjoyable, lasting friendships. It is a life where the mysterious, invisible link between us can be joyfully explored.

9

Submission and Patience

Faith doesn't mean that we always get our own way. To live a life of faith, we have to give up our way.

I have mentioned that in the years after I came to know the Lord, I received prayer at every opportunity for the healing of my feet. The healing never happened, but I was made to understand that if I just had the right attitude, if I had enough faith, it would have been done. This caused me to try hard to produce the right attitudes, words, and thoughts.

This view of faith—that if we can produce the right words and attitudes, it will make God do what we want—is destructive to authentic faith. It also doesn't seem to work.

Faith isn't something that we can produce by trying hard. It is a gift from God that releases His grace in our lives (Eph. 2:8). It's indispensable in the relational dynamic between God and us. Faith starts with our knowing the person of God. To have faith is to be convinced or persuaded. We're not expected to convince or persuade ourselves. We should be involved with God until His glory overwhelms us, convinces us, and persuades us.

When the disciples asked Jesus to increase their faith, He responded with a story that seemed to have little to do with the request (Luke 17:5–10). He talked first of faith as a grain of mustard seed. It can be small to begin with, but it has to be there and it has to be genuine.

Then Jesus tells the story of a man who works in the field all day. When the man gets home, his master doesn't wait on him because he has worked hard. Rather, his master sits at the table and he waits on his master until his master's needs are met. Even after this sacrificial service he recognizes that he's an unprofitable servant. He's just done his duty.

What? How is that an answer to the disciples' need for more faith? They had been seeing Jesus heal the sick and cast out demons. The Lord's powerful works got Him a lot of attention. They wanted to be able to do the same. Walking on water would be very cool. Raising a friend from the dead would surely make them famous and important. They wanted faith so that God would do those kinds of things for them. They would be valuable to others if they only had that kind of ability. They wanted Jesus to give them an impartation of power.

Jesus responds by telling a story that was shielded from the understanding of a casual inquirer. But He was pointing to an indispensable truth. It's something we must understand, or we won't grow in authentic, biblical faith.

We don't grow in faith by seeking to make God our servant. We grow in faith by waiting on Him as His servants and responding in obedience to His orders. That is what the servant in the parable did, and that is what we will do if faith is to be imparted to us.

As we spend that time, attentive to His desires, all that He is begins to infiltrate the fiber of our being. We begin to be one with Him. The oneness begins to be a reality in our minds and spirits.

He is in us and we are in Him. The Father is in the Son and the Son is in us and we are in the Spirit, who is one with the Father and the Son. His thoughts start to become our thoughts. His desires are becoming our desires. We respond to His desires with obedience, and we're changed. His life is flowing in us. That is growth in faith.

Sometimes miracles happen as a result. This depends a lot on the gifts, calling, and personality of the person who is growing in faith (1 Cor. 12:29). The manifestation is not the point. The point is that we are becoming one with the Lord and moving from glory to glory (2 Cor. 3:18).

This must happen not only in the prayer room but also by obedience when we leave the prayer room. It was not easy for me to go into the unknown of Brazil on one-way tickets with a new bride to care for, no visas, and six dollars in my pocket. It was, however, a necessary response to what God had said to us about His desire and will. Without obedience, faith is dead. Obedience is so much a part of faith that the two cannot be separated.

When I was eighteen, I left home to go to Bible college. I was impressed with the seriousness of a life in the ministry and felt like I should do something to show my commitment and develop my spirituality.

As soon as I arrived, I went to the library. I asked a girl on duty that day if she knew of any good books on prayer. She couldn't call any to mind, and I was about to leave in disappointment when another student came in and put a book on the counter. He was finished with it. The girl's face brightened and she said, "Oh, I think this is about prayer."

I checked the book out and began to read it. It was the diary of David Brainerd, an American missionary in the eighteenth century. This was a man who demonstrated a tremendous devotion to God and perseverance in prolonged prayer that could only have come through his experience of the Lord. He was a powerful man of God through whom unreached peoples were brought into the kingdom.

I was deeply impressed by how much time and effort Brainerd put into seeking God. Often he prayed all day and only broke through to God in the evening. He habitually had to pray through his own depression, wrestling for hours until he experienced joy. I had never prayed for more than an hour, and that was during an enthusiastic youth camp gathering. If I didn't feel some emotion right away, I would be off to do something else.

Later in Brainerd's ministry, the Lord poured revival out on the Native Americans that he ministered to. I wanted to have those same powerful results in my ministry. For that to happen, I would have to be a man of prayer like David Brainerd.

I set my alarm clock for five thirty the next morning. I got up and made my way down to the prayer room in my dorm. I had until seven o'clock. I knelt alone in a moldy basement without windows and began to pray. I asked God to bless my family. I asked God to bless our government. I asked God to bless my college and its leaders. I asked God to bless the missionaries. I was out of subjects, and only a minute or so had gone by. What would I do for the rest of the time? I didn't understand prayer. I approached it like I was giving God a shopping list or a list of tasks to be done. I thought that doing more of the same with greater force and determination would constitute faith. I didn't get it.

Looking at Brainerd's diary today, I'm amazed at how little I understood when I first read it. Here was a man who was a product of seeing God and receiving the gift of faith. He describes his conversion this way:

> As I was walking in a dark thick grove, *unspeakable glory* seemed to open to the view and apprehension of my soul. I do not mean any *external* brightness, for I saw no such thing; nor do I intend any imagination of a body of light, somewhere in the third heavens, or any thing of that nature; but it was a new inward apprehension or view that

I had of *God*, such as I never had before, nor any thing which had the least resemblance of it. I stood still, wondered, and admired! I knew that I never had seen before any thing comparable to it for excellency and beauty; it was widely different from all the conceptions that ever I had of God, or things divine. . . . My soul *rejoiced with joy unspeakable*, to see such a God, such a glorious Divine Being; and I was inwardly pleased and satisfied that he should be *God over all* for ever and ever. My soul was so captivated and delighted with the excellency, loveliness, greatness, and other perfections of God, that I was even swallowed up in him; at least to that degree, that I had no thought (as I remember) at *first* about my own salvation, and scarce reflected there was such a creature as myself.*

It's clear to see that on that day, David Brainerd received the gift of faith. He experienced the person of God. He was captivated and delighted with excellence and beauty. His experience of excellence, loveliness, and beauty was so great that he forgot about himself, absorbed in God. It was a relational and not a legal experience. His life of prayer came from that day, and it consisted of waiting on God until God took him in one direction or another.

Faith doesn't consist of having some sort of capacity to make God do things, some sort of legal demand. It is relational, exercised in an attitude of submission and patience. We offer ourselves to God in prayer, ready to listen, rather than talking all the time. As we spend time with God, waiting on and responding to His good pleasure, we are transformed. He also speaks to us about the world, and our faith begins to bring transformation to others.

---

* *Life and Diary of the Rev. David Brainerd*, in *The Works of Jonathan Edwards*, vol. 2 (Edinburgh: Banner of Truth, 1974), 319, available at http://www.ccel .org/e/edwards/works2.ix.i.i.html.

If we see faith as a mechanism through which we can control circumstances, we haven't understood it. Controlling circumstances through words and attitudes is the goal of sorcery, not faith. Faith has everything to do with yielding and nothing to do with dominating. The more we are drawn into the glory and wonder that is the person of God, the less we are in control, but we are ever more deeply engaged. This does not mean that He becomes more and we become less, as if we fade away as people. We are made in His image, and His intention is our growth. He shows us the glory, and in this process we are moving from glory to glory with Him (2 Cor. 3:18). His life flows out of this dynamic unity between Him and us and changes the world. It's not a process where God bypasses us, but rather a relationship where He fully engages with us.

Many times God doesn't do what we want Him to do. We ask, and He seems to go off in another direction. He wants to deal with us in a way that we haven't anticipated. It seems to us that He's not answering. Do we have the faith to move through these times with patience and hope? If we really know Him, we will wait and He will use the occasion of our need to deal with us and change us. Faith is about Him changing us and through us changing the world.

Faith is about yielding, not forcing the issue. It's about patience and trust. To see the end of our faith, we take the long view.

The centurion in Matthew 8 understood this and was a source of wonder to Jesus (Matt. 8:5–10). When he says Jesus had only to speak and his servant would be healed, his explanation seemed to be the opposite of exercising authority. He didn't emphasize that he could give orders. He emphasized that he was under authority. He had understood, and Jesus marveled. When we place ourselves in submission to Jesus, we discover our true identity. When we give up our drive to get what we want, He empowers us to pray with great boldness and release His will on earth as it is in heaven (Matt. 6:10). Faith is not about taking control but about becoming one with the relational, cosmic flow of what really is. We are immersed in God's will until He releases great victories in and through us.

It's not about Christian gnosticism, which dismisses the material as evil and therefore unimportant. God is generous and inclusive. If what we are experiencing is biblical faith, then it will engage the human need all around us. It will not center on us and make us selfish consumers of spiritual highs, merely looking for more experiences and thrills. Through faith God will transform us into compassionate, wise, and powerful people who change the world or die trying.

This "seeing" of God, the eyes of faith, motivates us. In Hebrews 11:27 we read this about Moses: "By faith he forsook Egypt, not fearing the wrath of the king; for he endured as seeing Him who is invisible." It's in the seeing of faith that we take up the cause of the kingdom, a better life for every person in the world.

Hebrews 11 speaks of many heroes of faith. Verses 33–35 talk of great victories won through it. Kingdoms were subdued. Justice was administered. Promises were obtained. The mouths of lions were stopped. Fire was quenched. The faithful escaped the edge of the sword. Out of weakness they were made strong. They became valiant in battle and turned to fight the armies of the aliens. Even the dead were raised!

Now that sounds like a robust, can-do, positive-thinking, active faith. That's what so many of us want. We think we can get a decisive edge in a competitive world so that our cars will be more luxurious, our houses bigger, our businesses more profitable, our health only good all the time, and so on. God will make us winners in such a way that the whole world can see it and be impressed! This won't work. God wants our transformation more than He wants to give us things. He will deal with our self-centered hearts and worldly desires. This is His priority and a life of faith begins with this dealing.

A full reading of Hebrews 11 shows us that people living by faith were not always visibly victorious. They were also tortured.

They were mocked and scourged. They were chained and imprisoned. They were stoned. They were sawn in two. They were tempted. They were slain with the sword. They were destitute, afflicted, and tormented. They wandered the face of the earth. Then, after all that, they did not get the promise.

What is the difference in the faith that is exercised by those who were triumphant and by those who suffered? There is no difference. It's the same faith.

The circumstances in which we live by faith are not the point. The point is to live in close friendship with God, experiencing and living by His life in us. We should not come to Jesus so that He will always and visibly make us winners. Winning is not the point. He is the point. Living our lives in Him and Him living through us is the goal. We must submit and be patient to emerge from the shadows of dead religion into the sublime light of Jesus.

Francisco, Part 4

Francisco was out of jail and waiting for government forces to arrive in Ganda. When the army finally swept into town, one of the first things they did was to seek him out and arrest him.

"You are a leader in the community," an officer told him. "The UNITA forces didn't kill you, so you must be one of their agents. The only way you can prove to us that you aren't an agent for those bandits is for you to kill some of their people for us. If you kill these people, we will believe that you are with us and not with them."

Francisco looked the officer in the eye and said, "The Bible is God's word. It says, 'You shall not kill.' I have to obey the Lord. I can't kill the people that you suspect of being sympathizers with Savimbi."

The officer yelled at him for a while and then locked him up with three other men in the same jail he had recently gotten out of.

A couple of days later, some soldiers came in and dragged two of the men out behind the jail. They took the prisoner's shirts off, pushed them down on their knees, and shot them in the back of their heads.

They left the bodies in the tropical sun for two days. The stench was becoming difficult to bear by the time they came in again. They dragged Francisco out behind the jail. One of the soldiers pushed him down on his knees in front of the corpses.

The officer joined them and took an AK-47 from one of the soldiers. He pushed Francisco over onto a body. He placed the barrel of the gun just below Francisco's ear and pressed hard until his face was right against rotting flesh.

"Do you see this man?" he asked. "If you don't kill the people we want you to kill, I am going to shoot you, and you will look just like him in a few days." Then he pulled back the action on his gun, getting ready to fire.

Francisco said, "Do whatever you have to do. I have to obey Jesus."

The officer pressed harder, his eyes bulging with fury. "I mean it," he said.

"I believe you, but I still have to obey Jesus."

The officer stepped away, lifting the gun barrel from Francisco's head. He looked frustrated and confused, but also impressed.

"I don't know why I don't kill you," he said. "But I am going to offer you something. We have gotten word that there is a man of interest to us at the market this morning. Take my gun and go arrest him. That will be enough. We won't insist that you kill anyone."

Francisco stood up and said, "I cannot take your gun. If I have a gun, he will see that as a threat to kill him. I'm not going to kill him, so it would be a lie. The Bible says, 'You shall not lie.' Is it acceptable if I just go and try to convince him to come and talk to you? If he won't come, you can do as you desire. If he does come, then am I okay with you?"

The officer agreed, and Francisco headed for the marketplace. He found the man and convinced him to come back to talk to the authorities.

The government officials now decided that Francisco was on their side, so they drafted him into the army. He wouldn't carry a gun, so they put him on guard duty. I guess they figured that at least he could yell if the rebels came into town during the night.

Things were going well now, but soon Francisco would face another life-and-death situation.

10

Strategy

Our faith is more than a personal journey. It results in unity and motivates us to engage with human need. As God's heart infiltrates ours through the exercise of our gift of faith, we become inclusive like Him. We become compassionate like Him. We become generous like Him. We become loving like Him. There is no room for indifference. We must act on behalf of God and on behalf of all people. Love that limits itself to me and mine isn't godly love.

For the last one hundred years or so, many Bible-believing Christians have tended to invoke a life of faith as a way to secure personal salvation. Faith is seen as a way to get to heaven. This can easily become a legal rather than a relational understanding of the process of salvation.

When Jesus taught the disciples to pray, He taught them these words: "Your kingdom come. Your will be done on earth as it is in heaven" (Matt. 6:10). It seems that God is concerned with getting heaven to earth. He's not content to leave the world to the devil. He wants us to battle to bring His will to pass here on earth.

He wants us to have the attitude involved in these phrases. We should never pray this way unless we are willing to get involved. This is not a mere nod to the human need in the nations, without involvement. It's also not something limited to religious concerns.

God is interested in agriculture because He is interested in children having enough to eat.

He is interested in government because He wants people to be treated fairly and justly, living productive lives of human dignity.

He is interested in the arts because He created and values beauty, story, and the deepest longings of the human heart.

He is interested in culture because it is the vehicle of people's values and beliefs.

He is interested in entertainment because, used wisely, it can be a vehicle for truth that can bring peace and wisdom.

He is interested in education because it informs the minds of impressionable children, doing much to set the direction of their lives.

He is interested in families because they are the builders and context out of which we receive and live our lives. He lives eternally in the family of the Trinity. He's even added a lot of adopted children. All reality is rooted in family.

He is interested in academic life because intellectuals create paradigms that shape the next generation through the artists.

God is even interested in our recreation because He enjoys it when we have a good time. He knows that it's important for our relationships and well-being.

It's not enough for us to win souls and plant churches all over the world. Jesus wants us to teach the nations to obey all that He has taught us (Matt. 28:20). He taught us that love, a commitment that aims at everyone having the chance to live a good life in every area, is the great commandment (Luke 10:27).

He wants us to be salt and light to all corners of human society. He wants women to be free of exploitation. He wants children to be safe from abuse. He wants working men and women to have decent wages that permit them to support their families in dignity. He wants marriages to be stable sources of love and security for children. He wants everyone to have a life of fulfilling productivity in serving others.

Faith will inevitably lead us to fight for the things that Jesus values. The more we dwell in His presence, the more we become co-participants in His nature. We can't stay aloof and still have intimacy with Him. He will guide us with His eye on us as He brings us to engage with His concerns.

Some of us will do small, simple undertakings. Some of us will be involved with large, complex projects. To the extent that these efforts come from His life in us, and to the extent that they conform to truth, they will be vital, relevant, and transformational. If we walk by faith, they will be an authentic outcome of our partaking of His nature.

God alone holds the overall strategic plan. We are not capable of containing such complexity and wisdom. He will share details with us, individually and corporately, and guide us to do certain things. We will understand enough of what He shows us to obey, but we won't understand all the complexities of how our part interacts in synergism with the other parts.

We are helped, though, by having an overview of God's intentions. The sort of wisdom we need cannot come only from the visible, physical world. We need a more complete understanding. We must go beyond the epistemology of the Enlightenment and have a more complete way of learning, understanding, and knowing. We need to learn directly from God.

We humans have used the rigorous thinking of scientific endeavor to progress in science and technology. In this material reality it is wise to insist on proof, but while we are moving ahead in technology, we don't seem to be making the same progress in ethics and morality. With humanity so involved in behavior that harms others, technological progress is a mixed blessing. Advanced technology in the hands of evil people is dangerous.

The deepest problems of the world come from broken relationships, out of control appetites, lust for power, greed, dishonesty, unspiritual religiosity, and so on. The wisdom and power to solve these problems can only come from God. We won't have victory unless we walk by faith and Christ lives in us. How much more do we need faith in our corporate efforts, aimed at achieving God's purposes on earth?

If we don't come out of the prayer room and apply what He teaches us, we cut off our unity with Him. If we don't use the wisdom He imparts for the good of others, our lives of faith will not last. We gain intimacy with God not only through prayer, meditation, and worship but also through doing things with Him.

He has told us to pray that the good things of the kingdom of God may come to the world (Matt. 6:10). When we work with Him on fulfilling His desire to see this happen, our oneness with Him increases. We begin to see not only His actions but also His ways of doing things (Ps. 103:7). We weave a common history with Him of what we have done together. This common history becomes a profound, intimate, and irreplaceable reality. This mutual involvement is as much a part of our life of faith as is our prayer.

It is a remarkable thing that God called me to belong to the wonderful tribe of Youth With A Mission. This belonging has been a great source of blessing, including wisdom, emotional and spiritual support, mutual understanding, and strategic faith. The life of faith is seen in the Word as a life in unity with others. We live this out in formal and informal circles of friendship. God has no intention that we should develop our lives of faith alone.

Living strategically by faith is a vast subject. Faith is for personal salvation and growth, but it is also for the transformation of nations. We must not divorce one from the other, or neither will work the way God wants it to.

What is the goal of a life of faith? What should the outcome be?

This life will, of course, work on an individual level. We live by faith, and as a result love and power are released in our lives as a direct expression of our union with God's life. This is not just religion that seeks to gain a legal standing with God. It is a relational response to God Himself that produces His life in us. We become co-participants in the divine nature (2 Pet. 1:3–4). This not only takes care of our guilt as we appropriate Jesus's death in our place, but it is also a solution to our wickedness as His transformative power is released in us. Old things pass away, and all becomes new (2 Cor. 5:17).

Francisco is an example of the power of this sort of life. He lived through great suffering but also lives in great joy. It is evident that he draws from an outside power, an invisible source, the fountain of love, wisdom, and power.

We can all have that power. As a matter of fact, the New Testament is written in the certainty that we will all walk in that power. For instance, the book of 1 John considers no other possibility. Everything comes as a result of our encounter with Jesus, and the one who is born again doesn't walk in sin.

This power is not to be confused with fame, wealth, position, or any other common foundational condition of coercive or manipulative capacity. This power is Jesus in us. His presence is invisible, but it is overwhelmingly effective.

Jesus's message was the gospel. However, in the Scriptures his message isn't described with just that one word. It is almost always written that Jesus came preaching the *gospel of the kingdom*. The good news isn't just that we can get saved, but that He wants to bring all His goodness to all creation. He's for us and not against us.

This kingdom is spiritual in nature. We can't see it if we aren't first born again (John 3:3). That new birth is a divine initiative. It is outlined in Ephesians 2:8: "For by grace you have been saved through faith, and that not of yourselves; it is the gift of God." It involves God making Himself known to us, and in that knowing is the gift of faith. With that gift comes saving grace. To participate consciously and intentionally in promoting God's kingdom, we must have a life of faith.

However, that personal experience and reality needs to lead to involvement with the gospel that is not just personal. It is the gospel of the kingdom. Prophecies and proclamations that deal with the birth of the Messiah often give emphasis to His kingdom.

In Isaiah 9, for example, the prophet says that the government shall be upon His shoulders. He is called the Prince of Peace. The prophet declares, "Of the increase of His government and peace there will be no end."

When the Lord announced Jesus to Mary, He said, "The Lord God will give Him the throne of his father David. And He will reign over the house of Jacob forever, and of His kingdom there will be no end" (Luke 1:32–33).

Jesus's birth involved much more than individual salvation. We need to receive faith and intimacy from God to fully participate. The gospel of the kingdom is meant to produce more than a scattering of individuals who participate privately in personal salvation. The term "kingdom of God" requires coordination and corporate expression through divine government.

This is a government moved only by pure love. This is a kingdom of grace. Its lines of authority are invisible to the natural eye because they are spiritual. Everyone in the kingdom has access to the King. The unity of this kingdom (John 17:9–11, 20–23) is beyond our capacity to describe. Here in John, Jesus prays that we might have the same unity between ourselves that He and the Father have. As we are in Him and He is in us, we are also one with each other. What a kingdom this is! It's like no other.

The first chapters of Luke deal with the time surrounding the birth of Jesus and vibrate with great excitement and anticipation of the coming of this kingdom. That humble beginning in the manger was filled with the certainty of great things to come. This was the beginning of an invasion. God's kingdom was coming to earth! Jesus was the second Adam, the beginning of a new humanity. All things were to be made new. Old things were to pass away. This wasn't an opportunity for some to escape the corruption of the world. This was a plan to bring heaven to earth.

The New Testament is primarily about this eschatological context. God has plans to change all of creation. His kingdom will grind the glory of the nations to dust so fine that the wind will blow it away (Dan. 2:44), and His kingdom will grow and fill the earth.

How will the nations be ground to dust? This won't be in the normal way we think of destruction. The weapons of our warfare are not carnal but spiritual; they break down strongholds opposed to God. Love and wisdom will reduce to nothing the normal way that empires do things. The destructive ways of empires and earthly powers will prove vastly inferior to God's kingdom. That kingdom will finally replace them entirely. The intrinsic value and true glory of the peoples will be freed as the evil power structures are brought to nothing.

You might object that these things are too great for us. You would be right. However, Isaiah 9 predicts this level of victory and speaks to the source of it. It says, "The zeal of the LORD of hosts will perform this" (v. 7). That's how!

We can't fix everything in the world. If we embark on such a course, we will exhaust ourselves. We will become frustrated. We will lose our love and become harsh and demanding. The complexities will overwhelm us. We will never be able to accomplish it. What we can do is concentrate, individually and corporately, on Him. We can make sure that we do the one necessary thing. Then we go from that place, individually and corporately, and obey. Our faith lives. God is released. His plans and dreams are fulfilled. His kingdom keeps increasing.

At some point Jesus will return and visibly take the helm. Meanwhile, we are to occupy this world that He has given to us, making "disciples of all the nations, baptizing them in the name of the Father and of the Son and of the Holy Spirit, teaching them to observe all things" that He has commanded us (Matt. 28:18–20).

In order to develop and grow in a life of faith, we need to get on board with this plan that God has for our world. We can walk by faith, individually and corporately. We can walk in intimacy with Him. We can obey what He speaks to us and what He shows us. We can increase in knowing Him, moving from glory to glory. He can become in us everything we need (1 Cor. 1:30–31).

Here there is hope. We leave things that are beyond our comprehension to Him. We put our trust in His overarching understanding. We trust in His promises. We know that we can't do this, but we also know that the zeal of the Lord of hosts is up to the task. If we walk in Him, His power and wisdom will do through us what we could never do by ourselves.

Faith is how we participate in this greater strategy and in these amazing purposes. This seems to be the way the kingdom of God is unified and coordinated. We know and do our individual and corporate parts as He guides us.

11

The Word

When I met the Lord that night at the old tabernacle camp meeting, I didn't know much about Scripture. The church I had been raised in didn't believe the Bible was anything more than Hebrew literature. When God gave me faith that night, the people in Danny's little church were overjoyed, and one of them gave me a book called *Living Letters*. It was a paraphrase of Paul's epistles in modern English. Right after that my mom and sisters returned home from their time in San Francisco, and we went to a family reunion.

While we were there, I had good fellowship with my aunt and uncle, who had been praying for me. More indelible in my memory, though, is how I devoured that book of Paul's letters. It was like it was alive to me! Whenever I read, I could feel spiritual warmth in my inner being and was keenly aware of life flowing from God to me. I believe that this was foundational in nurturing me as a brand-new Christian.

If we are to live by faith, the Bible says we will do so only in the context of the living word of the Lord. The word of God is so much more than just a document. The Bible speaks of the word of God in at least three ways.

John 1 records beautifully the Word and His involvement in creation since the beginning. It speaks of Jesus as the Word, the Logos (John 1:1–17). The Logos was present at the beginning and made all things. Out of the Logos flowed life, and the life became the light of men. The Logos became flesh and dwelt among us. Moses brought us the law. The Logos, Jesus, brought us grace and truth. This is the first, eternal Word of God, the continuing Word of God that will endure forever as the Word. This Word is a person.

After Him came the Scriptures. All Scripture is inspired by God and is useful for applying in our lives (2 Tim. 3:16–17). The Scriptures have human authors, but Scripture finds its essence as that which is breathed by God. God inspired the Bible, and we can completely depend on its truth.

Hebrews 4:12 says that the word of God is living. In 2 Corinthians 3:6 we see that the letter kills but the Spirit gives life. It becomes evident that what is written lives through the Spirit. We should, through the Spirit, let the word be what it says it is—alive.

In 2 Corinthians 3:1–6 we see that we become living epistles for the whole world to read. As we dwell with the eternal Logos in the Scriptures, He teaches us regarding all things. This works a transformation in our lives that writes His word on our hearts, and we become an expression of His word as well. We're not some sort of religious salespeople or kingdom marketers. We spread life and light through His life and light in us. It is a transparent and authentic process. It's a way of life.

When I look back, I can see that during my time at Bible college, the word that we focused on was almost exclusively what was written. We believed in and honored the Scriptures as inerrant, but we treated them as a document to be dissected and analyzed. We didn't treat the Bible as an organic whole. We didn't approach it as a living, dynamic word. When we studied, we did so by going to the Bible to find propositional truth. We didn't specifically invite the participation of the Spirit. We weren't trying to find the Logos, who is the truth (John 1:17; 14:6). When we found ideas, we removed them from the narrative flow and plugged them into our thought systems. We used Enlightenment presuppositions to process all of this. In so doing, it seems to me that we killed something. We didn't let the word live.

One of the pivotal issues in pursuing my life by faith has been how to relate to, dwell in, and live by the living word of God. I think this question is of vital importance.

When I first came to YWAM in 1972, I had no concept that this potential to let the word live existed. I could study up a storm, but I never had any expectation of divine involvement. To me, Bible study was an academic or intellectual exercise. I felt comfortable and safe within this paradigm. I could research, organize, write, and present the ideas of the Bible, but there was very little life happening in the process. As a matter of fact, I was growing colder and more distant in my relationship with Jesus. This got so bad that it was a cogent factor in my ending my time at college very distant from God and deciding to backslide.

I soon saw the futility of trying to run from God. I couldn't get rid of the conviction, the faith that He had given me. It was too real and wasn't just a matter of my personal preference. Finally, I gave up and recognized that no matter what had happened, I still believed because He had revealed Himself to me. I got to YWAM full of hope.

The classes were very much focused on experiencing the life of Jesus in the context of the Scriptures. We were to meditate and hear God speak. We were to ask Him what He wanted and then pray accordingly. We were to ask Him for guidance in our actions and then go out and obey what we had understood from Him. Many of our classes were about interacting with our living, speaking God. This was a new paradigm for me.

It seems to me that much of the time we present-day Christians focus on having the right bundle of ideas. Propositional truth is the grand and often exclusive measure of the correctness of our Christianity. We aim to have accurate thoughts. We generally go to the Bible to seek out ideas rather than a person.

John 1:17 is instructive here: "For the law was given through Moses, but grace and truth came through Jesus Christ." The law came through Moses. The law was true. The law was accurate. The law defines God's character for us. The law defines love for us. The law is a mirror that convicts us of how different we are from God. The law is perfect and excellent. However, the Bible here makes a contrast between the law and truth. It seems that the law doesn't bring us to the beautiful, living, powerful truth that the Bible is talking about. It doesn't contradict, but it falls short.

What is truth? God's hope of truth in our lives isn't reached through understanding of accurate ideas. Truth is a person. The roots of reality are grounded in relationship. Loving interaction is the essence of ontology, of all that is. Nothing less than that loving interaction is sublime or complete enough to receive the title of truth. Many things are true, noble, and good, but they don't represent the holistic reality God wishes us to experience as truth.

Ideas are important. They are indispensable. Life is built around them. However, you can add up as many propositional truths as you want and still not experience the grace and truth that come through Jesus. That grace is His life shared with us.

Often an accumulation of facts about God seems to produce an ugly and aggressive spirit of moral and ideological superiority. We easily become sure that we have an unassailable grasp of right and wrong. We use that conviction to judge everyone who doesn't have the same bundle of ideas we have. The Spirit of Christ is lost. Life doesn't flourish.

I suspect that God is not impressed with the quality of our ideas. Still, we will grow. We will learn. Our ideas will change and get better. And while we're on earth, what we do not know will always be more than what we do know. Ideas are important but not decisive in their present state of definition.

The Lord is, however, insistent that you must be connected. The book of 1 John talks about the changes that happen when we are born again, when our spirits connect to God. This connection to Jesus will correct the misconceptions we have and elevate good ideas in our minds and hearts. The connection of loving relationship is the one thing that is necessary. This connection goes deep. We live in Him and He lives in us.

John 14–15 says beautiful things about our fellowship with God, but this connection goes beyond being linked to the divine. In John 17, Jesus prays that we would be one with one another as He is one with the Father. Such profound insights are sometimes beyond our comprehension. We get some of it, but the rest is a mystery that we can profitably explore forever. This evokes a deep sense of wonder and infinite potential. Only by our relational interaction with the Spirit of God can these relational depths become reality to us. They are the essence of living by faith.

Our interaction with the Bible will give us good and true ideas and concepts. But that is not all that it will give us.

What if we let the Bible live? What if we come to it with the expectation of finding the wondrous, sublime, holistic reality of truth that is in John 1:17? What if we approach it seeking connection to the eternal, personal, living word? What if we apply the resultant instruction to our lives in obedience? Then we will not only know correct ideas but experience the glory and wonder of deep connection with Jesus and with one another.

Our lives will be full of ongoing and living instruction from the Holy Spirit (John 14:26; 16:13). We are all unique individuals. We have unique DNA, unique histories, and unique families.

We have made unique choices and gotten involved in disobedience to God in unique combinations of circumstances and actions. We have unique gifts, strengths, and weaknesses. Only God completely and reliably knows all of this about us. Only He knows what it has ultimately produced in our hearts (Jer. 17:9–10).

To live by faith in a living relationship with the Word of God is to live in a flow of grace. We enter into the flow of His grace by faith, and we continue in the ways of grace and victory as we live by faith. It is a powerful result of walking in the revelation of His person and making this continuous gift our ongoing focus.

We can, "according to the riches of His glory, . . . be strengthened with might through his Spirit in the inner man" (Eph. 3:16). Christ can dwell in our hearts through faith (3:17). We can "know the love of Christ that passes knowledge" (3:19). The process of grace in our lives starts when God forgives us through Jesus's sacrifice on the cross. After we are in His embrace, a vast array of resources come alive to us and we are changed.

We're saved not only from our guilt but also from our sin. It's faith alone that does this. Biblical faith is authentic life that starts with God's initiative in giving us the underserved gift of knowing Him, seeing Him, experiencing His glory and light and life. It's Him making His word come alive to us and applying it in a personal way. It's Him instructing us individually with total understanding of our entire being and the wisdom that only He has to transform us. This gift is His grace, and out of this gift flows the transformation of our nature (2 Pet. 1:3–4).

Francisco, Part 5

Freed from jail and torture, Francisco was now in the army.

Not long after he was forced to enlist, a routine army patrol came back into town from patrolling the surrounding region. They had big news. By now the war was once again causing serious hunger in Ganda. Supply lines were disrupted, and people were beginning to starve.

The army patrol had discovered a large field of sweet potatoes ready to harvest. Taking the potatoes would supply the immediate needs of Ganda, but it would also take resources from the followers of Savimbi who had planted it.

The decision was made. They rounded up three hundred civilians and told them to be at the marketplace at four the next morning. They were to bring sacks with them.

The large civilian group assembled in the predawn darkness and began the walk to the field, which was thirty kilometers from Ganda. Fifteen soldiers escorted them. Francisco was one of the soldiers ordered to go. The group arrived at the field at about eight in the morning; the commandant told everyone to dig as fast as they could and to fill their gunny sacks with as much as they could carry.

Francisco's nephew was with the civilians. When they arrived at the field, he came to Francisco and said, "I saw movement in the bush. I think this is an ambush."

Francisco believed him, but there was nothing the two of them could do. Their hearts filled with apprehension, but they couldn't leave.

As the people spread out and began to harvest, the commandant placed his soldiers on the perimeter to guard them. Then
he threw a sack at Francisco and said, "You won't carry a gun, so
make yourself useful. Dig some sweet potatoes for me."

Francisco said, "Sir, I am a follower of Jesus. His word is the
Bible. In the Bible it is written that we are not to steal. Someone
planted these sweet potatoes. They are counting on them to feed
their families. I'm sorry, but as a follower of Jesus I can't steal
them."

The commander responded with fury, knocking Francisco
to the ground with the butt of his rifle. He kicked him and yelled,
"That's it! You will die right now!"

At just that moment everyone heard the wail of incoming
mortar rounds. Men opened up with machine guns from their
hiding places in the forest. The commander was the first to be
hit and fell dead at Francisco's feet. There were explosions everywhere. People were screaming and running. It was hard to see
anything.

Francisco jumped up and there was his nephew, Paulino,
who had come to find him. "Run!" Francisco shouted over the
mayhem.

They fled that place of death, running through the dust and
smoke of the explosions and the screams of slaughter. They kept
to as much thick brush as they could, but almost right away they
came to the edge of a wide-open space. It had been burned off to
prepare another field for planting. There was no place to hide.

Francisco and Paulino looked at each other. Could they break
cover? Would they be immediately shot down? But there was no
alternative. Staying where they were meant that they would certainly be found and killed. At least there was a small chance they
could make it across the open space. They ran.

Fifty yards in, Francisco had his legs blown out from underneath him. He couldn't get up, so he yelled for Paulino to keep

running. After he saw that his nephew had made it to the cover on the other side of the burn, Francisco took stock of himself.

He discovered that his legs were fine, but he had been shot in the foot. It looked bad, but in his desperation to get away, he managed to get to his feet. He couldn't walk. The wounded foot wouldn't hold his weight.

As he stood there, balanced on one foot, an overwhelming weariness came over him. He was so tired of fighting death that he started to think, *Why don't I just stand here and let them find me? Maybe they will take me prisoner instead of killing me. I don't think I can go on.*

Deep down he knew they wouldn't take him prisoner. They had no provision for such a thing. What would they do with prisoners? They had caught them taking their food, and there would be no mercy. Wouldn't it be like suicide if he just stood there? Would Jesus approve of that?

As Francisco stood there in indecision, a voice spoke to him. "Just lie down and stay very still."

Francisco lay down and stayed very still, while gunfire and mortars were still raging.

He saw a woman run into the clearing, looking for a place to hide. She ran to a bunch of thick brush that hadn't burned and burrowed in under the foliage.

A man also made it that far. He found a burrow that an animal had dug and managed to squeeze into it until he was completely hidden underground.

The sounds of the slaughter died down, with occasional bursts of gunfire as the guerillas found survivors. A group swept into the clearing where Francisco was lying still, out in the open.

He watched them search the brush and find the woman hiding there. They dragged her out and shot her in the back of the head. Then one of them saw the burrow and got down on his knees to look into it. He saw the man's foot, grabbed it, and dragged him out. The man's shirt looked pretty good, so they made him take it off. Then they made him lie face down on the ground and shot him in the back of the head.

Francisco was waiting his turn, but the rebels never saw him. They kept going, searching everywhere for survivors. He lay there until about one in the afternoon and then dragged himself to cover. There he found a stout branch and fashioned a staff for himself. He hobbled on that all day and into the night. He got to about ten kilometers from Ganda. At that point, he passed out. Someone found him and used a wheelbarrow to take him back into town. Only sixteen people made it back alive that day.

Now that Francisco was wounded, it didn't look like he would be a suitable soldier anytime soon. The army discharged him in November. He started working at evangelism, as he had learned from our team. By May he had led seventy-three people to the Lord and didn't know what strategy to use in discipling them. He made the dangerous trip down to Benguela to ask Marcos what he should do. That's what led to my meeting him there and hearing this story as he and I and Paulino crouched in the darkness of the backyard.

When Francisco had finished telling me his story, I wanted to know how he had felt as he lived out this fearful drama. I asked him, "When you were in the hole, waiting to be buried alive; when you were lying on the corpse, waiting to be shot; when you were lying in the field, waiting to be found and executed, what did you feel?"

He gave a huge smile and said with transcendent joy, "Oh! I felt so good!"

Francisco isn't a masochist. He wasn't faking. He was relating an authentic experience of receiving the joy of God's outpoured grace in response to his obedience of faith. Hebrews 2:14–15 says that Jesus was incarnated so that "through death He might destroy him who had the power of death, that is, the devil, and release those who through fear of death were all their lifetime subject to bondage." Despite all the anguish and suffering of his country and his town, Francisco was free. Nothing in this world could subject him any longer to bondage. He was free from the fear of death. Everything else is a lesser fear. Perfect love had cast out fear. What amazing freedom! To walk by faith is to walk toward this perfect freedom.

Here is a man who literally would rather die than steal some sweet potatoes and disappoint Jesus.

Most of us don't have to face the horrendous conditions that Francisco did. Most of us don't have to decide between surviving and following Jesus in obedience. In this, our lives don't look like Francisco's at all.

Yet we all face the same essential challenge as Francisco—the challenge of faith. Will we live in the flow of God's powerful life in us, or will we try to do it on our own? Will we find the same joy, freedom, and power as Francisco?

12

Miracles

Once I had to fly from Belo Horizonte in the center of Brazil to Manaus in the Amazon. To get there I was to connect through Brasília. I got up early and left home at five thirty in the morning. I caught my flight and we took off for Brasília.

I was reading a book and was soon engrossed in the story. There were a lot of announcements during the flight, but I wasn't listening. Our landing in Brasília was rough and I took notice. The guy next to me had his camera out and began taking pictures of the runway. This was when cameras still had film, and his was motorized, so I heard the distinctive sound as he rapidly recorded the scene.

I looked out the window to see what his focus was. All along the runway there were fire trucks and ambulances. By now the plane was braking sharply and had started to go a little sideways. Finally we stopped, still on the runway and without injury to anyone.

It was only as the crew began to organize us to leave the plane that I realized we had made an emergency landing. We had circled above Brasília, dumping fuel and preparing. Announcements had been made to ready passengers, but I wasn't listening, engrossed in my book. The plane's hydraulic system had failed. The pilot had shown great courage and ability in landing without a crash.

The plane wouldn't taxi, as the wheels were locked up. They brought a bus out on the runway, and we departed the plane and were taken to the terminal. The airport shut down because our plane was in the middle of the runway. I knew this would make the midday news, so I thought I'd better call Pam and let her know that I was okay.

When she answered, before I could say anything, she asked, "What have you been doing?"

"What do you mean?" I said. "Have you been watching the news?"

"The news?" she asked in alarm. "What do you mean?"

I explained to her about the flight and our emergency landing.

"That's amazing," she responded. "Today at breakfast Adriana came and told me that I wasn't to worry, that you would be fine. I asked her what she meant, because now I was worried. She said that the Holy Spirit had awakened her at four in the morning and told her your life was in danger. The Spirit asked her to intercede for you, and she did so until the sense of danger had passed and she was assured that you would be okay."

We were amazed and full of joy as we realized the Lord had intervened to save my life. We were glad that one of our team members was so attuned to Jesus that she could hear and obey His call to pray. The miracle was on both sides, God talking to her and the actual saving of the plane and its passengers. These were miracles of guidance and deliverance from death.

Once I was visiting an isolated tribe in the Amazon. We had two YWAM workers there and were making a pastoral visit. We stayed about five days. I had my hammock in the *maloca* (house) of the tribal chief.

Each evening the people of the village would gather to hear me teach the Bible. I was impressed with how much they responded with understanding. I thought they had a good grasp of Portuguese and of spiritual things.

Soon after we departed to continue our missionary journey, some of the people came to Marcia, one of our missionaries there. They asked her where she had found a foreigner who spoke their language so fluently. She told them that I didn't speak their language at all.

They wouldn't accept her explanation and told her that I had taught them fluently every evening in their tribal language. I was unaware of what was happening, but while I was speaking to them in Portuguese, they were hearing in their own language. This was a miracle of teaching and language.

Not all of us will be involved in the same sorts of miracles. As we walk by faith, we will tend to manifest miraculous power in the area of our gifts and callings (1 Cor. 12:27–31). I, for example, will probably never be a charismatic and famous healing evangelist, but God does teach supernaturally through me. Another might be able to practice hospitality at a level that will bring supernatural edification and grace to many. We are not to covet others' gifts. We can all walk on a supernatural level, releasing the life of Christ to a lost generation.

Miracles happen every day all around the world. Jesus taught that faith could move mountains. When He performed miracles, He often spoke of the faith of the one who received the blessing.

When we were newlyweds, Pam and I had an opportunity to go to hear Kathryn Kuhlman, a famous healing evangelist, in Los Angeles. We saw many impressive miracles that day. It was amazing. I especially remember a young woman who arrived in an ambulance and was carried in to the meeting on a stretcher. She was painfully thin.

During the meeting Ms. Kuhlman pointed toward a section of the auditorium and said, "God is healing a young woman of cancer right now somewhere in this section. Please come forward and tell us about it."

The young woman jumped from her stretcher and ran up the long ramp to the stage. She was crying and laughing at the same time and saying, "I'm not going to die. I'm not going to die." This was a moving miracle of healing.

Striking miracles like that one happened all afternoon, but Kathryn Kuhlman kept saying over and over throughout the meeting, "The greatest miracle of all is when one soul comes to Jesus."

She was talking about the new birth. She was talking about Ephesians 2:8, when God makes Himself known to us, giving us faith. His grace then saves us as we respond to His presence. This is where miracles start, and it's where our participation happens.

A miracle isn't a violation of reality. It isn't a breaking of natural law. It is, rather, the invisible, spiritual realm exerting its greater power over the physical, material part of reality. The spiritual is as real as the material. It has been around for a lot longer than the material. It is substantial. It exists objectively and is not dependent on our beliefs or impressions. God, the great I AM, resides in the invisible, and everything comes from Him. The material came out of the spiritual, not the other way around.

Yesterday I was listening to an interview of an author who discoursed on the conflict between religion and rationality. She associated words like *ignorance* and *superstition* with religion. She associated progress and the future with science. This happens a lot all around us in our society. Faith and science are presumed to be contradictory. They are, of course, not contradictory at all.

A materialist sees things that way because of the conceit of thinking that only material knowledge is true knowledge. If this is true, then everything that goes beyond the material is superstition and is irrational. It's just a vestige of humanity's ignorant past.

Those who live by faith know that there is more than just stuff. They know that science is a wonderful way to deal with the material, but they never forget that reality includes more than that. They are living in harmony with the way things really are.

The Bible doesn't see it as strange or unusual when the spiritual universe intervenes and exerts control over the material. In the Scriptures we don't find long, philosophical apologies for miracles. They are quite natural, a logical outcome of the nature of things. After all, creative activity out of spiritual reality is what happened in the creation of the material universe. That's how all that we see around us came into being. This creative activity continues today through the lives of those who walk by faith.

Once we were holding a Leadership Training School in a Muslim region in Asia. During the course, we had a well-known American Bible teacher who was giving wonderful classes. I wanted him to have more contact with the students, mostly locals who didn't speak English, so I arranged a special lunch with him and several students.

At first there was little interaction. The language and some cultural norms were preventing most conversation, so I asked each of the students to tell the teacher about some expression of the power of God in his or her ministry.

The first student told of how when he was just starting out in the ministry, he had gone off into the jungle to preach the gospel in villages. When he came to the first one, the people asked him not to speak of Jesus to them. He asked them why, and they took him to the edge of the village. There was a man, chained and shut up in a bamboo cage. The villagers explained to our student that this man had demons. Whenever they did anything that this spirit didn't like, the man would burst his bonds, break the bamboo cage, and go on a rampage, destroying the village. They were sure that this would be his reaction if they permitted the gospel to be preached there.

The young man didn't give up. He headed for a nearby mountain and established a camp at the summit. He fasted and prayed for two weeks, using oil lamps to light the darkness of the long nights.

At the end of two weeks, evil spirits came during the night, blowing out the lamps and plunging everything into darkness. He literally wrestled with them through the night. As dawn approached, he prevailed in the name of Jesus and the spirits departed.

He came down the mountain and cast the demons out of the caged man, who returned to his right mind and began to converse. When the villagers saw the power of the gospel, they welcomed the message of the young evangelist. This was a miracle of deliverance.

We went around the circle, and there were many testimonies of the manifest power of God.

One of the most powerful came from the leader of a tribal group. His people lived in a village in the jungle, and they had all become Christians. One day as they sought Jesus, God poured out revival in their village, and they advanced mightily in the life of faith.

On one occasion they were praying over a national disaster in their country. An oil well had caught fire. The country had tried with its own experts, but they couldn't put it out. They then called the biggest experts from Asia, but to no avail. Finally, they called the most recognized expert in the world. He couldn't solve it either. His equipment would melt from the heat before they could get the machines close enough. The country was covered in a pall of black smoke, and the national wealth was burning away.

As this little group out in a forgotten village in the jungle prayed, God spoke and told them to put the fire out. They were perplexed. How could they do this? They didn't know, so they asked the Lord what they should do. What would the first step be? He told them to seek an audience with the leader of the oil company. They obeyed and arranged a meeting with his wife.

It turned out that this woman was a believer, and she arranged a house close to the well fire where they could pray. The house was within sight of the inferno, and there was a stream between the house and the fire.

The band of unknown tribal members began to pray in the house. They prayed through the night, and as dawn approached,

God asked them to go outside. They lined up along the banks of the stream and extended their arms toward the roaring light of the flames. As the Lord led them, they commanded the fire to cease and be still. As soon as they did, the fire began to diminish and went out entirely!

What all the experts couldn't do, God did through anonymous people who knew how to walk by faith!

I later visited the country where the fire had happened, and I looked it up in the media records from those days. Before that night the news of the country was full of depression and perplexity. No one had any answers. After the little team prayed and the fire was overcome, the newspaper and other media avoided any detailed explanation of what happened. This is a strongly Muslim country. What were they going to say? In the end, they just talked in general terms about how in unity anything is possible. It was clear as I read through the accounts that the solution had been sudden, unexpected, and mysterious to them.

This was a miracle of biblical proportions. It was a prophetic sign that God is the Lord and Jesus is the Messiah.

The last testimony at our luncheon was from a little guy. He was thin and not at all impressive in his stature or appearance. He and his team were involved in planting churches in a Hindu region.

There was a village where only one woman would talk to them. One day a small team was in her home teaching her about the Bible when she suddenly jumped to her feet, clutching her chest and showing great distress. She staggered around the small living room and fell out the open door onto the ground outside. The team rushed to her and checked for a pulse. There was none. They tried to resuscitate her, but to no effect. Twenty minutes or so went by, and they saw no signs of life. They found a mirror and put it to her face, looking for any fogging that would indicate breathing. There was no fogging.

Finally, the leader sent the other two team members to find the woman's husband and call him home. The leader didn't want to abandon the body, so he stayed back. More time passed, and he had even stopped praying.

As he thought about this circumstance, he began to get angry. He was sure that no one in the village would want to hear anything about Jesus for the foreseeable future. They would conclude that this woman had died because she had shown interest in a foreign god, and their local deities had risen up to kill her. They would be terrified that the same thing would happen to them if they listened to the Christians.

These thoughts were unbearable to our team leader. Trying to rekindle hope, he went over and opened one of the woman's eyes to see if it would react to the light. There was no reaction, and he knew that she was dead. What could he do?

Greater anger rose within him. It was intolerable that this woman's death would condemn a whole population to live without the gospel of the kingdom. Recognition began to grow in his mind. This refusal to tolerate the situation was coming from God.

When he was confident of this, he stood to his feet and commanded the woman to arise. She stood up, alive and well! This was a resurrection miracle.

The American teacher who was with us at this lunch meeting appeared to be impressed by these and other testimonies. I guess he thought that he had to say something as well. He told us that once they had called him to pray for a woman who had suffered much through many years of chronic illness. He prayed for God to end her suffering. He asked that the Lord either heal her or take her. She died on the spot.

He said, "That was a miracle too!"

I told him that indeed it might have been, but that if I were ever sick, I would rather they call the other people around the table and not him! We all laughed.

In Matthew 13:58 we read, "He did not do many miracles there because of their unbelief" (HCSB). The people's unbelief on that occasion was a result of their familiarity with Jesus and his family. This was Jesus's hometown, and they couldn't believe that the man they had seen grow up could be all that special. Their unbelief blocked the miracles.

Today we face a deeper unbelief than was present during Jesus's life on earth. We have taken Darwin, Freud, Enlightenment epistemology, Marxist materialism, and the thoughts of many others to develop an explanation of the universe and humanity that doesn't require a creator.

These views fall short in explaining reality, and in my opinion don't bear much examination. But so many people want to be free of restraint and to be their own gods that they eagerly latch onto them. These theories dominate formal education all over the world. A huge vocabulary and vast complexity have been developed to the point that it becomes difficult for young students to untangle everything and get to the root issues. We hear these theories thousands of times, and they become woven into our consciousness. A life of faith becomes difficult when one has been indoctrinated in the belief that faith is a thing of the past and that progress comes only through materialistic rationalism.

You can hear the unease in many Christians when they make apologies for acting in faith. Deep down we often feel that faith is irrational. We say things like, "Sometimes you have to take a leap in the dark." Or, "Sometimes you have to leave your mind behind and trust your heart." These are phrases from people who know the spiritual dimension but have not learned to appreciate the coherency of a life of faith. A life of faith reflects what really is. A life that only recognizes and gives weight to the material is incomplete and leaves out the most important reality.

Perhaps this is one of the reasons we see so few miracles in the West and among highly educated Christians all over the world. Their teachers have indoctrinated them away from faith.

These impediments can be overcome, but it will take a conscious effort and a lifestyle of immersion in the living Word. I would also suggest that we get teaching from people around the world who have never become as divorced from spiritual reality as we highly educated people have.

Nothing has changed in the basic reality of the universe. Miracles still can and do occur every day all around the world. These miracles usually go unremarked in public discourse and we don't often hear of them. This can leave us with the impression that miracles are no longer happening, but that is a misapprehension. As we walk by faith, we can become part of this wonderful and ongoing divine intervention on the world's behalf. It should be a vital part of our witness.

Once when we were in Indonesia for some months, Pam made friends with a Muslim woman. The woman practiced Islam with diligence and zeal. Her children were up every morning at four o'clock so that they could dress, do their ceremonial washings, and be ready for the early call to prayer. The family observed Ramadan, a yearly month-long fast, together.

Over a couple of months the woman became fascinated with us and with our message. One day I asked her if she wanted Jesus.

A look of great longing came over her face and she said, "Oh yes. I want Him, but I don't want to offend Allah. I need a sign so that I can know for sure that this is truly the right way."

We don't know what has happened to that woman and her family since then. On the day of our conversation, I was left feeling completely inadequate. Why couldn't I release the power of God in a miracle that would have shown the true way to this woman? I don't know. What I do know is that if we live by faith, the volume and power of miracles will increase and multiply around the world. Let's pursue that outcome.

13

Provision

Although God is often presumed to be interested only in religious matters, this is not the case. He's about life and light. He's about love and the character needed to sustain loving relationships. He's about friendship and beauty and grace. He multiplied fish and bread for the multitudes. He grilled fish over the fire for his disciples. His care extends to our daily provision.

While Jesus cares about our daily needs, He also warns us about making things the focus of our lives. In Matthew 6 He exhorts us to trust the Father for our provision, telling us not to be anxious about what we will eat or what we will wear. He says we must lay up treasures not on earth but in heaven. He points out that we cannot serve both God and Mammon, or riches. The beginning point for us to understand how faith relates to our daily provision is to let the Lord purify our hearts from the love of riches.

In 1 John 2:15 it is written that if we love the world and the things that are in the world, then the love of the Father is not in us. This is not a question of pretending to not love money so that we can get more leverage with God in the hope that He will give us more of it. This is a relational question, one that is at the heart of our authentic love for God. How can we develop our faith, a relational process, if we don't love the Father?

We also have the famous passage from 1 Timothy 6:10: "For the love of money is a root of all kinds of evil, for which some have strayed from the faith in their greediness, and pierced themselves through with many sorrows." Please don't skip over this part in order to get God to help you with your finances. You can't pull the wool over His eyes.

So many passages in Scripture instruct us about these things. In Colossians 3:5, for example, we discover that covetousness, the cousin of greediness, is idolatry. This will result in many sorrows in your life.

God will test you on this. If you respond by being generous and obedient, then your faith will live and life will flow. If you respond by withholding what God is asking for, then He stops and waits for you to obey before He moves on to the next thing in your spiritual progress. He is not going to feed the love of money in your life by giving you more of it before you deal with this idolatry. He puts more priority on your freedom and transformation than on your possessions. This is not God asking for something difficult of you just to see if you will do it or not. This is our loving Father working with you to set your heart free from the love of Mammon.

He wants you to be free. Once you are, He can pour out abundance in your life as an outgrowth of your growing faith and an expression of His love for you.

It seems to me that this issue is more problematic and more central to our faith than we often recognize. I have visited and ministered in hundreds of churches on every continent of the world. During these journeys, I've visited lively, faith-filled churches. I have also been in churches that seemed cold and evidenced very little life. What is the most common difference between the two? One might think that it would be the worship, or the high quality of Bible exposition, or the development of community and a strong sense of belonging for members, or any number of other things. In my experience, though, the central issue is often this freedom from the love of Mammon. Almost always, generous churches have a lot of life and love. Churches that are not generous have little life and love.

Why would it be different in our individual lives? God wants to bless us with provision, but first He must set us free. We need to cooperate fully with Him in this process.

When God called me and Pam to Brazil, we were severely tested on these things. We arrived in Brazil with six dollars in our pockets, a promise of fifty dollars a month support, and not even an address where that support could be sent. We definitely weren't going for the big bucks. It would take miracles, a lot of them, to see our daily bread supplied. We were called by God to enter into the same battle on the same level that the yet to be recruited Brazilian missionaries would face as we fought to generate a missions movement in a nation that had yet to recognize its role in reaching other nations.

Sometimes the challenges were moderately big. Mostly they were small because we didn't have enough money to get into the big ones!

Once we needed money to pay our room and board for the month. We had about forty dollars but needed another hundred. I didn't want to spend even a few cents for the bus fare, so I walked downtown to get our mail. Upon arrival I opened our post office box to see what we had.

There was an envelope from Hawaii with the name of a good friend on the return address. When I opened it, there was a note and a hundred-dollar bill.

The note said something like this: "Hi Jim and Pam, I was working at my job at the Honolulu Airport. It was my turn to take care of the conveyor belt for the garbage. I just kind of watch and make sure that there are no blockages or spillage from the belt. As I was watching, a hundred-dollar bill went by in front of my eyes. I could not believe it! I turned it in to lost and found, but no one claimed it. Today it was returned to me. I prayed and had the impression that God wanted me to send it to you guys immediately. Do you think that I really heard from God?"

There was a hundred dollars in my hand! It came on the very day that we needed it. I don't know how God placed it on that conveyor belt, but He most surely intended it for us. I'm sure that our friend heard from God, and I wrote to tell him so.

God had told us to go to Brazil, even though the resources didn't seem to be there. We obeyed Him because of our faith in Him, and He came through with provision. That faithfulness on His part encouraged us and deepened our relational attachment to Him. Our faith lived and grew.

I walked home rejoicing, and we paid our room and board. We were penniless again, but we hadn't failed in our financial commitments. God didn't deliver us from our complete dependence on Him for funds. We needed this walk of faith. The future Brazilian missionaries needed us to have these challenges together with them. Looking back, I'm amazed at how much God trusted us with those difficulties. It's very humbling.

A year or two later we attended leadership conferences with Loren Cunningham, Joy Dawson, and Brother Andrew as the speakers. Bethany Fellowship was sponsoring the meetings, and our little band of YWAMers was helping out, serving in any way we could. There were to be three weeks of meetings, one in Belo Horizonte, one in Rio de Janeiro, and one in São Paulo.

During the first week in Belo Horizonte, Loren spoke on the role of finances in the life of leaders. He emphasized obedience and generosity in our financial lives. To provide an opportunity for people to immediately apply the message, he took up an offering. Loren is a man of the highest level of integrity. He wanted all motives to be transparent. He decided to give the offering to Youth for Christ so that neither Bethany nor YWAM would be seen as having a hidden agenda. The agenda was to obey the Lord.

I was sitting in the front row when the offering bag was passed around. As a result, I was one of the first to receive it and hadn't finished receiving guidance from God. I put a little in and the bag went on its way. I immediately lost my peace and knew that I should have put in all that I had. That's what the Lord was asking of me.

I prayed, "Lord, if you give me access to the offering, I will put in all that I have."

As soon as I finished praying, the director of Youth for Christ, who had just been presented with the offering, turned to me and asked if I would count it.

I was excited that my prayer was answered so directly. As soon as I had the offering, I slipped the rest of what I had into the pile. I was so full of joy.

The meeting ended, and it was time to go home. Now I was face-to-face with our circumstances. We had been getting to the meetings on city buses. I was paying the fare because the other YWAMers had no money. How was I going to tell them that I had just given away our bus fare and that we had no way to get home?

As I was beginning to work myself into an anxious state with these thoughts, a young volunteer came up to me. Her name was Eliza, and she had come from Argentina to serve with our team.

She extended her hand, and I shook it as she said, "When I prayed about what to give in the offering, I felt like God told me to give nothing. I was, instead, to give this amount to you."

There was something in the hand that I was shaking. When she walked away and I opened my hand, I found the exact same amount of money that I had put in the offering! I was amazed at God. I now had a way to get everyone home.

The next week we were in Rio. Members of our small team were staying all around Rio. I was sleeping in a bookstore. Two of our team were bunking in a sort of halfway house for recovering drug addicts. The others were in various other places.

Each morning, before the meetings started, we would pray together and organize our activities for the day. We didn't have enough money to eat a proper restaurant lunch, so at midday we would go to a bakery and buy bread and milk. These two items were inexpensive because the government subsidized them. The bread was like little loaves of French bread. The milk came in plastic sacks. We would take the food to a nearby park and eat bread and milk, tearing the sacks open with our teeth and sucking it out of the bags. This was not a dignified process.

Eliza, the volunteer from Argentina, had brought her unsaved sister along on the trip. Her name was Dina. One day as we sucked on our milk sacks, Dina got angry. When we arrived back at the church, she was feeling humiliated and spoke roughly with Eliza and me, insisting on better conditions. It wasn't a pretty scene.

Before each teaching session in these conferences, I would meet with the leadership team for prayer. Loren Cunningham was always there. He is the founder of YWAM and one of the men I most look up to in the world. Joy Dawson was always there. She taught us to walk in constant, real contact with the Lord. She taught us to pray by first hearing what God wants us to pray. She was a major influence in teaching me to really live by faith. Brother Andrew was there. He impacted the attitude of the worldwide church in caring for closed countries. He went where no one thought we could go. He broke the barriers of unbelief over the unreached people of the world. What a man of God. George Foster was there. He was a dear friend and great man of God. He and his wife, Dolly, had befriended Pam and me and were so important to us as we struggled to adapt to a new nation.

In other words, I tried to be as quiet and unobtrusive as I could when praying with that group. I didn't want to mess up in front of these people!

On that day, I went to the prayer meeting immediately after the contentious scene with Dina. When I kneeled to pray, I felt an impression that I should pray for Dina. It was a specific impression that I should pray for her to be born again. It also included the detail that I should pray for this to happen on that very afternoon.

I silently explained to God that Dina was angry and not at all in a mood to give herself to Him. I told Him that Joy Dawson would be listening to my prayer. What would she think if I prayed and nothing happened? I said to Him that Loren was there and was just forming his opinion about our ministry in Brazil. What would he think if I prayed these wild prayers?

God wasn't convinced. I continued to feel that I should pray, with all the details. Finally I did pray, out loud for all to hear, that Dina would come to Jesus that very day.

Joy spoke that afternoon. I think the subject was unity, but it didn't seem to have anything to do with Dina getting saved. At the end of the teaching, Joy made an appeal for people to go to each other where there had been any kind of break in relationship and to reconcile with each other. A pastor from the city of Campos came to me. I was listening to him but also trying to see where Dina was and wondering what was happening with her. It didn't seem probable that my prayer would be answered.

When the pastor and I finished talking and praying together, I went looking for Dina. I found her at the back of the cathedral, collapsed in the lap of Eliza and crying with brokenness and joy. She had been born again. God had made Himself known and given her the gift of faith. Grace was flowing. She serves God to this day.

Provision isn't only physical. Man shall not live by bread alone.

On Friday of that same week, God asked me to bless our two team members who were staying at the halfway house. It was a very specific blessing. I was to take them out to Brazilian barbecue on Saturday before we traveled on to São Paulo.

This made no sense to me. We were eating bread and sucking milk out of plastic sacks for lunch. We needed bus fare to get to São Paulo. How could I spend money on an extravagant meal for the three of us? I explained all of this to God, but again He wasn't convinced.

The persistent sense of His guiding wouldn't leave me, so on Saturday I took the two workers out. They seemed inordinately happy with their churrasco. Their smiles were almost splitting their faces. Finally, I asked why they were so joyful.

One of them said, "In the place where we stayed, they didn't feed us. The only food we had all week was the bread and milk at lunch. We didn't want to complain, so we stayed quiet. We prayed together, though, and asked God to give us churrasco on Saturday. It seemed so impossible. Now here we are, eating our churrasco and rejoicing in God's care for us."

I was so glad that I had obeyed the Lord in this small thing. Occasionally, the process of faith in provision involved larger amounts.

A couple of years later we were finally on our own property. Things were very basic, and we were years into trusting God day to day with the provision of our simple food. Many times we went to bed at night, not knowing where food would come from the next day for our forty workers and children.

In the middle of these circumstances, I was on a trip to Southern California to speak at a missions conference. The host church had been a real partner to our ministry, helping us in our building program. One day the leadership team called me to a meeting. When I walked in, they had silly grins on their faces and seemed anxious to say something. The upshot was that they had sold some land and were giving a tithe to YWAM Brazil. The amount was twenty thousand dollars.

I was astounded. I had never had so much money. Immediately I started imagining the improvements we could make to our living conditions and the extra space to increase the number of missionaries.

However, when I later stopped to pray, I put the money on the altar. I submitted it to the Lord and asked Him what we should do. The answer brought me no immediate joy. I felt that the bulk of the money was to go to a new initiative in the city of Belém, in the delta region of the Amazon. This pioneering work was just starting, and they had committed to buy a property. We were to help. It looked like a sacrifice, because we really needed that money. The joy of obedience and living faith soon came, though, as we gave most of the money to Belém. Our circumstances stayed the same, but our faith grew as we unselfishly served the purposes of the Lord. That work in Belém later became the source of initiatives all over the Amazon, with many people coming to the Lord and whole regions experiencing revival. What an investment!

Our base in Belo Horizonte went on to become a large sending base, spreading initiatives among many nations. Would we have done as well if we had kept the money rather than obeying? It seems a sure thing that closing the circle of faith with our obedience was much more important than money. Our faith lived and produced results all over the world.

————

Let's return to Francisco to see his experience of God's provision. We didn't touch on it the night that I talked with him in the backyard, but later I heard the rest of this story from Marcia.

During the year of the truce, our team in Angola received, besides food, containers of items donated by generous people in the body of Christ in Germany. Occasionally, a container that should have gone somewhere else found its way to Ganda instead. This led to some funny situations, like Marcia trying to explain ice skates to people who had never seen ice, not even an ice cube!

In one of these containers there was a pair of brand-new boots. They were made mostly of rubber and more suited to Europe than the interior of Africa, but they were good boots. Marcia asked God what to do with them and understood that she should give them to Francisco. So she did.

Instead of using the boots, Francisco asked the Lord what he should do with them. He felt like God told him to put them away. He did as God asked. He never used them.

Time went by. The year of truce came to an end, and our team of Brazilians was forced to leave Ganda at gunpoint. Francisco was left behind, and I have told much of that story. Great suffering returned to Ganda, and the population became desperate to flee the war.

A man came to Francisco and made a proposal. He wanted to leave Ganda with his family. There were no means of transport available. He would have to walk, but he didn't have a good pair of shoes. How could he walk to the coast across the thorny and stony interior? He had heard people talking about Francisco's boots and he wanted to buy them, but he didn't have any money. The only thing he had that he could trade was his farm.

At the time, no one knew when the war would be over or who would win. It was unclear whether there would even be private property if the Marxist government won. Archives of land titles didn't exist for Ganda, whose infrastructure had been destroyed as the war swept back and forth over the city.

Given the situation, this man thought that the boots were more useful to him than the farm. Francisco asked the Lord what to do and felt he should make the trade. The man left town, striding out comfortably in his new footwear.

Having the farm meant nothing when this happened, but over time the government prevailed and won the war. Things started to settle back to normal. People started to plant and harvest again.

Francisco's claim to the farm was officially recognized, and now he is a property owner. His life of faith was strong enough to face death without wavering. He was so determined to obey God that he wouldn't steal a potato to save his life. The same life of faith gained him a farm.

God recognizes no separation between provision of our daily needs and provision of our invisible, spiritual needs. It's all from the same faith. It's all a result of our relationship with Him. It's all fruit from the same tree. In a life of faith everything dwells in the bright light of God's care for us.

14

Love

When I was a young man in college, I desired power from God. I think that I had a genuine motive to make an impact for Him, but it was mixed up with other motives. I wanted to be famous. I wanted to be recognized. I wanted to be successful. I wanted to have prosperity in the ministry. Power itself had a seductive allure. I wanted a way to avoid problems and tragedies in my life. If I had power, I would never have to be sick, in need, or struggling with failed relationships. I could just exercise control through the power of God, and my life would be pleasurable and free of sadness and anxiety.

In seeking after this controlling power, I thought God would be more likely to give it to me if I sacrificially earned it. Fasting was a way of getting my way with God. Prayer made certain that God would answer. Generosity was tied to having God multiply money back to me. I made great efforts to believe by exercising my willpower, trying to reach a level of faith that would obligate God to answer. Living a sacrificial life on the mission field would surely give me some currency with the Lord. The more difficult something was for me to do, the more weight it would have in getting God to attend to my desires.

God fights against these attitudes. All the letters that Paul and the Holy Spirit wrote to the churches were centered on countering these transactional, legalistic approaches to religion and to dealing with God. Galatians 3:21 says, "If there had been a law given which could have given life, truly righteousness would have been by the law."

I never got any life from those attitudes, and I never got any power. Neither does anyone else.

It is not overstating the case to say that most people try to exercise control to get what they want. They do this in every dimension of life. This gives rise to actions and practices that violate love in the name of personal happiness or pleasure. This often happens universally before people know the Lord, but it is also prevalent among those who know Him but don't walk by faith.

If we know the Lord but don't continue in a life of faith, we will avoid the gospel, the church, and Christians altogether, or we will slip into attempts to do things of virtue that we can then use to get God to do what we want. It's the same spirit of control. It's the same independence. It's the same pursuit of personal desires above everything else. It's just expressed in pious terms and has the added dimension of the seduction of a feeling of moral superiority.

This seems to be the default position for humans in religious matters. If a powerful and positive force is not exercised in another direction, this is where we go. We want what we want, and if someone convinces us that religion will help us get it, then we'll use religion.

At least we try to.

Happily, God is not subject to our manipulation. His goals are radically different from the normal human way of doing things.

He's going for disinterested benevolence. In God's universe, love governs life. Faith only works through love.

This being the case, when we try to use God's power for our own advantage and put personal advantage above the well-being of others, we violate the very foundations of biblical faith. It won't work. Formulas don't work. God doesn't submit to our attempts at control.

He is not interested in us proving that we're winners. He's not concerned with our attempts to show that we are more competent, intelligent, and powerful than others. He sees our insistence on control not as an answer but as a major impediment to His goal of transforming us into the image of Christ. He won't negotiate with us, allowing us to use our perceived virtue as the currency of power. He's not impressed with our will-driven attempts to have faith.

He does, however, want to pour out "the exceeding greatness of His power toward us who believe, according to the working of His mighty power" (Eph. 1:19).

In Ephesians 3:16 Paul prays that God "would grant you, according to the riches of His glory, to be strengthened with might through His Spirit in the inner man." What are we strengthened for? Why does God promise to strengthen us?

Paul continues praying "that Christ may dwell in your hearts through faith; that you, being rooted and grounded in love, may be able to comprehend with all the saints what is the width and length and depth and height—to know the love of Christ which passes knowledge; that you may be filled with all the fullness of God" (Eph. 3:16–19).

Faith and love cannot be separated. If we don't allow Christ to dwell in our hearts through faith, we will never be rooted and grounded in love. We will know nothing of the surpassing knowledge that is only experienced as love. We will never know what it is to be filled with all the fullness of God.

This dimension of faith and power only works through love. God will work out these questions in us. He will discipline us

(Heb. 12:6). He will pursue us. He will pour out His love in our hearts through the Holy Spirit (Rom. 5:5). He will become for us wisdom—and righteousness and sanctification and redemption (1 Cor. 1:30). He will give everything we need for life and godliness through our knowledge of Him (2 Pet. 1:3). He will apply His great and precious promises to us until through them we become co-participants in the divine nature (2 Pet. 1:4).

These are promises that fill us with wonder. We are to receive exceedingly great power from Him and live it out in a lost world.

None of it will work except through love.

We need to know God to the point that our selfish ambition is swept away by wonder as we gaze upon His glory and excellence. We need to dwell in the bright white light of His presence if we are to overcome darkness in our hearts.

Our fear compels us to control things to avoid disaster and unhappiness. We need to experience throughout our lives the perfect love that will cast out fear and set us free to love.

Our natural desires motivate us to treat others as if their value is in giving us what we want. We need to dwell close to the overwhelming wonder of God Himself, until He is the sum of our desires.

We lack wisdom. We need knowledge of the ways of God. A life of faith is a life that draws constantly on the Holy Spirit to teach us all things.

We need to know our own deceitful hearts better so that we can respond with confession and repentance. Only God has the necessary understanding to help us with this as we walk by faith (Jer. 17:9–10; Ps. 139:1–6).

We need genuine belief. A life of faith is a life that comes from abiding in Him and results in the authentic conviction that only He can impart to us.

Only when these processes are active in our lives are we going to live the power that is promised us. Power without love is destructive.

We must go to Him. We aren't good sources of the love that we need. He is the source, the only source. A life of faith is a life of power. A life of faith is a life of intimacy with God. He is love. He is a consuming fire. As we dwell close to Him, that love will burn away the things that are a violation of love.

Neither rules nor regulations nor doctrines nor dogmas nor disciplines nor rituals will do any of this for us. The Bible is categorical: "The just shall live by faith" (Hab. 2:4; Rom. 1:17; Gal. 3:11; Heb. 10:38). There are no other options that will produce this love and power in us.

Second Timothy 3:1–5 is a sobering passage about the state of the world during the last days. There is a grim list of ways that people violate love. Much of it is seen in our times. We find the final item in verse 5: "having a form of godliness but denying its power." Then we are exhorted, "From such people turn away!"

We need to question ourselves. Are we living a form of godliness but denying its power? Have we bowed to the supercharged unbelief of our times and reduced our expectations to a self-help religion of human techniques? Are we the sort of people that others should avoid? Do we fail to live the power of the gospel through faith? Are we living far, far below the potential of "Christ in us"?

The promises for everyone who lives by faith are clear, and there are a lot of them. This ambition is so high that God aims at our "bringing every thought into captivity to the obedience of Christ" (2 Cor. 10:5). He goes so far as to promise that we will be co-participants in the divine nature (2 Pet. 1:4).

Please don't give up on God's ambition for your life.

Don't pursue it with the religious prohibitions mentioned in Colossians 2:20–22. "Don't touch this" and "don't handle that" will get us nowhere. They don't work. Verse 23 of the same chapter says that these things are of no value against the indulgence of the flesh.

Pursue God's ambition for you by abiding in Him. Pursue Him. He is the way, the truth, and the life. He will become love and purity and power in you. Only one thing is necessary. Let's choose the better part.

Everyone is at some specific point in the development of their faith. Some are farther along than others, but where you find yourself right now isn't so important. What is important is that you comprehend the nature of a life of faith and that you begin to proceed from glory to glory (2 Cor. 3:18). In whatever place you find yourself, seek God to be able to move ahead to the next level. He will guide you. Don't go back to a life lacking divine power.

I leave you with the words of the Holy Spirit, written through the agency of Paul: "I . . . count all things loss for the excellence of the knowledge of Christ Jesus my Lord, for whom I have suffered the loss of all things, and count them as rubbish, that I may gain Christ and be found in Him, not having my own righteousness, which is from the law, but that which is through faith in Christ, the righteousness which is from God by faith" (Phil. 3:8–9).

May you have a rich and fulfilling life, and may God find in you "the riches of His inheritance in the saints" (Eph. 1:18).

Acknowledgments

This book has been the result of teamwork. I want to thank Pam for her encouragement and support. The diligent and skillful editorial work of Ryan Davis and Luann Anderson were fundamental to bring the finished book to birth. Thanks to them. Our staff at the base where we currently live and work in Curitiba, Brazil, shouldered a heavier burden in order to allow me to take out big blocks of time to write. I'm grateful to Francisco for the life of faith that he has lived. Most foundational of all was the Holy Spirit. Jesus promised that He would teach us, and He does. Thank you to the whole team.